FARUK DİL

YUNUS EMRE

His Life, Perspective, and Poems

Copyright© 2021 by Faruk Dilaver

All rights reserved. This book or any part thereof may not be used in kind or in summary or otherwise without the express written permission of the copyright holder.

Published by Dilaver Yayıncılık
Ankara, Turkey

First Edition 2021

ISBN: 979-871-39333-4-0

Dilaver Yayıncılık
Mürsel Uluç, mh. 991.sk. No:17/B
Dikmen, Ankara, Turkey

FARUK DİLAVER

YUNUS EMRE

His Life, Perspective, and Poems

CONTENTS

CHAPTER ONE 13
LIFE AND PERSONALITY OF YUNUS EMRE 13
- "DO YOU WANT BREATH OR WHEAT?" 15
- MOURNFUL YUNUS 31
- HUMBLE YUNUS 33
- LOVER YUNUS 35
- HIS WORKS 37

CHAPTER TWO 41
PERSPECTIVE OF YUNUS EMRE 41
- PRESENTATION 43
- HIDDEN TREASURE 45
- CREATION OF HAZRAT ADAM 53
- WORLDLY LIFE 57
- DEATH 67
- THE AFTERLIFE 71
- OUR RELIGION AND OUR WORSHIPS 75
- PRAYER 101
- SUFISM 105
- THE PERFECT MAN 117
- KNOWING YOUR NAFS 129

CHAPTER THREE 139
INTERPRETATIONS OF YUNUS EMRE'S POEMS 139
- THE TRUTH CREATED AN ORE 141
- I LOVE YOU WITH ALL MY HEART 143

KNOWING YOUR ESSENCE	145
THOSE WHO COME TO THIS WORLD	147
IF BOTH WORLDS BECOME A DUNGEON	149
KNOWLEDGE IS TO KNOW THE KNOWLEDGE	151
IF YOU ARE TRUE LOVER	153
O LIFE, YOU DECEIVED ME	155
THE MAN OF LOVE, OPEN YOUR EYES	157
THE ONE KNOWING THE ORIGIN OF THE WORDS	159
SACRIFICING YOURSELF FOR LOVE	161
THE ONE DIVING INTO THE SEA OF LOVE	163
GRASP LOVE	165
TELLING WHAT ONE DESERVES	167
I WALK BURNING	169
I AM NOT HERE TO STAY	171
YOUR LOVE TOOK ME AWAY	173
THE ONE WHO REPROVES ME	175
WHOEVER NEEDS A TRUE FRIEND	177
IF YOU SEE THE WAY I DO	179
EVER SINCE I LOVED YOU	181
YOU ARE MY DEAREST	183
HERALD THE LOVERS	185
YOU ARE CLOSER TO US THAN OURSELVES	187
I WALK ALONG THIS PATH	189
LISTEN TO ME EVERYONE	191
NEVER SET YOUR HEART ON THE WORLD	193

THE ONE WHO CLAIMS TO BE IN LOVE	195
LOOK INTO MY HEART	197
MY EYES AND MY HEART	199
O FRIENDS, O BROTHERS	201
THE POOR MANKIND	203
ASK THOSE WHO KNOW	205
SUFFERING AND HARDSHIP COME FROM YOU	207
GOD WILL SEND TO YOU	209
I WAS WALKING TO REFRESH	211
SINCE I DIVED INTO YOUR WISDOM	213
THE SPIRITUAL WORLD CAME TO MY HEART	215
FRIENDS OF GOD CAME WITH LOVE	217
DO NOT SETTLE FOR A LOOK	219
I CAME TO THIS WORLD ALONE	221
LISTEN, THE ONE ASKING OF ME	223
BECOME ONE	225
GOD GAVE ME SUCH A HEART	227
PROPER WORDS	229
I SPENT THIS LIFE FOR NOTHING	231
I FOUND THE ONE WITHIN ME	233
DESTINATION OF THIS PATH IS FAR	235
THE DRINK FROM THE TRUTH	237
BE A SERVANT TO A SULTAN	239
STATE OF THIS WORLD	241
IF YOU ASK ABOUT THE TRUE FRIEND	243

I USED TO TRAVEL ON THE EARTH	245
THE STATION OF LOVE IS SUPREME	247
GOD! GIVE ME LOVE	249
I SPENT MY DAYS IN VAIN	251
IF YOU NEED A LESSON	253
O FRIEND! THE FIRE OF YOUR LOVE	255
THE GRAVEYARD IN THE MORNING	257
IF I TELL YOU MY SECRET	259
EVERYBODY TALKS ABOUT MY LOVE TO YOU	261
I PUT MY FACE ON THE GROUND	263
ABSENCE AND POVERTY	265
HEAR ME, MY FRIENDS!	267
DON'T YOU REMEMBER THAT DAY	269
WHEREVER I TURN TO	271
HOW MAY I HIDE THAT I LOVE	273
LET'S ASK THE SOULS	275
THE ARROW OF LOVE	277
THE ONE ASKING FOR THE TRUTH	279
FOR THE SAKE OF THE TRUTH	281
O, BEAUTY! BE GENEROUS	283
I AM IN A WONDROUS STATE	285
COME ON, MY HEART!	287
MY LOVE FOR THE CREATOR	289
MAN OF MEANING ON THIS PATH	291
IF YOU LOVE THE LOVE	293

IF YOU'VE MET A MIGHTY PERSON	295
I CRY FOR THE TRUE FRIEND	297
ABOUT THE AUTHOR	299

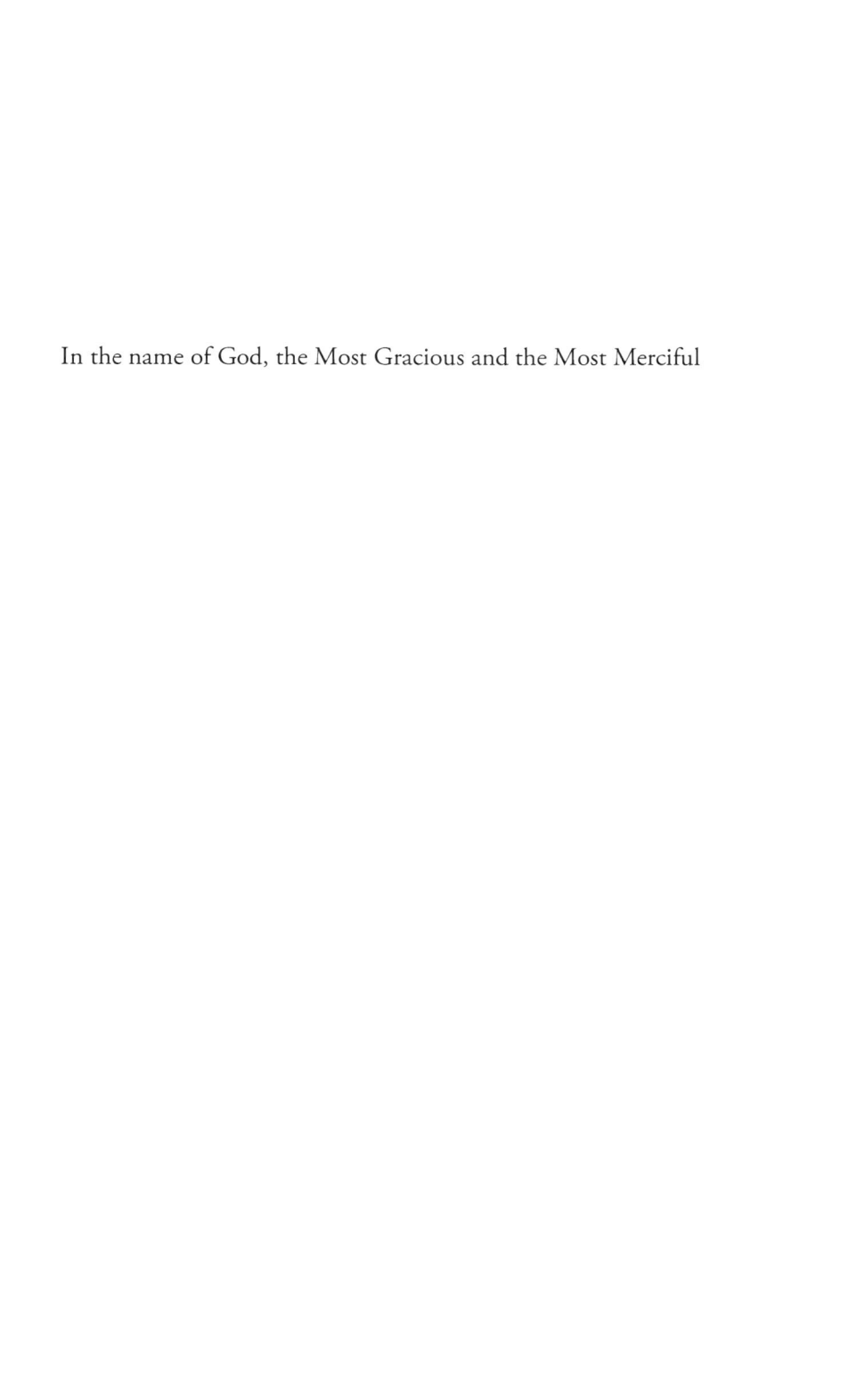

In the name of God, the Most Gracious and the Most Merciful

CHAPTER ONE

LIFE AND PERSONALITY OF YUNUS EMRE

"DO YOU WANT BREATH OR WHEAT?"

We have very limited information about Yunus Emre's life. The most important resource about him is his poems. The years of birth and death are generally accepted as 1240 and 1320. It is important to know about the era when Yunus Emre lived in order to understand his personality and poems better.

In mid-11th century, the borders of Great Seljuk Empire which was founded in Khorasan reached up to Anatolia. The Byzantine Empire which was ruling over Anatolia at that time initiated the Crusades to cast away the threat by Turks. The Seljuks won the battle against the Crusades and conquered Anatolia. In time, the Great Seljuk Empire gave place to Anatolian Seljuk Empire. The Crusades continued during that era as well. Although Turks won several victories in those battles, both Anatolia got devastated and the state seriously weakened. People of Anatolia were attacked by the Crusades in the West and by the Mongols in the East. Mongols reached up to Sivas in 1231, killed the majority of the people, and they left before the army arrived. They were repeating these attacks from time to time. People were feeble because of the Mongol occupation, and they gathered around their own leaders due to lack of protection by the state. The process where the seigniors became stronger and the unity was disrupted began. The seigniors battled with Mongols on one side, and with the Seljuks on the other.

Eventually, Anatolia was dominated with numerous social disturbances with occupations, revolts and establishments problems, and local unrests. Anatolia became a hot spot with the Crusades, Mongol raids, various revolts, and fights for the throne.

The era which formed the personality, poems, and the spiritual life of Yunus Emre was a very chaotic period in which people incurred great sufferings. Yunus Emre spent his life, spread his ideas, and made effort to establish unity and solidarity in Anatolia. He visited all seigniors and provided a great service by explaining them the importance of uniting.

We mentioned earlier that we do not have precise information about Yunus Emre's life. However, we will try to briefly tell about Yunus Emre's life based on what we compiled from his poems and epics written about him:

Yunus Emre was born in a small village named Sarıköy located at the junction of Porsuk Creek and Sakarya River. He lost his father at a very early age and left alone with his mother. Like many people who lived in Anatolia at that time, they subsisted on farming.

Yunus Emre was a young man loved by the villagers and appreciated for his respect, manners, and dignity. He was born and grew among such pure people whose entire world was that small village and only purpose was to work to sustain their lives and perform the worships they were ordained. Although he hadn't seen anything beyond these, he always thought to himself that there was something missing. He felt uneasy and he was on a quest. He was trying to find the remedy to his problem and to appease that uneasiness without knowing what he was searching for or what that remedy looked like. Sometimes he was so overwhelmed that he immediately walked away from everyone and everything and ended up in graveyards. There, he felt he could breath and he got even a little closer to what he was searching for; he was thinking for long hours, but he was not able to work it out. He was looking at the graves and he was unable to understand. He thought, "So that we will die, why were we born into this world? Every person arriving this world should have a mission, and this mission should not be such simple things like feeding, marrying, and reproducing." Because even the animals could do these.

Yunus began to keep the suffering of unknown reasons within himself even as a youngster, and as his grievance increased, loneliness became his friend, and he became a friend to the miserable. Anyone who had a problem visited him, and they felt a strange relief upon sharing their problems with him. He constantly supplicated the Created and asked for remedies for their problems.

He was longing. He was longing for someone or something that he didn't know. A yearning which burnt his heart, which he couldn't tell anyone...

His mother was very concerned about that state of Yunus. She was crying thinking whether he fell in blind love or smote upon taking a wrong step; she was inquiring in vain without getting any answer.

Time passed by and life went on while Yunus was struggling with his problems. That year, there was a very little crop, and the bins were almost empty. And winter came on top of it. The entire village was struggling with hunger, cold and despair. Many elders, patients, and children died in misery.

The notables of the village gathered and decided to send someone among them to Hacı Bektash Wali's village which they heard to be a land of milk and honey. Because when everyone was struggling with famine, the abundance in that village was the talk of the town.

Yunus immediately volunteered to this challenging duty. He wanted to be alone, travel, and see new places; he thought he could ease the suffering he felt inside.

The other day, Yunus set off on the ox-driven cart provided by the villagers by leaving his sad mother behind. On his way, he thought: "As per our traditions, I should bring a present but there was nothing in the village to offer as present..." Just then, he noticed the thorn apples by the road, and he got off the cart and picked some thorn apples. He put them into his bag and continued to walk. Now, he felt comfortable.

Yunus was on his way. He walked day and night. He stopped by several hostels as he moved. He met many people at every stop. He listened to different miracles and beauties of Hacı Bektash Wali from each one; but what he heard were irrational and unreasonable. Yunus didn't lingered over those words. His concern was to reach his destination as soon as possible and quickly turn back to his village with wheat, if they gave. Because every day he delayed was a great loss. His mother and the villagers would starve.

He finally reached Hacı Bektash Wali village. He had seen many villages struggling with famine and shortage on his way, while that village was in abundance. The entire village was verdant. The village welcomed people with a smiling nature with flowers all around.

Yunus couldn't believe what he had seen. He was lost in amazement!

He asked the harvesting farmers about the lodge of Hacı Bektash Wali. They stopped working and brought Yunus there. They thought they might see their Sultan with this occasion. Yunus didn't understand that either. What was the secret of the Sultan that made people stop doing their works to see his face for a couple of minutes?

When they reached the lodge, they were welcomed at the door. He was friendly invited to enter in beyond all questions. Yunus immediately started to tell his problem. He briefly explained that his fellow villagers were starving, and after kissing the hand of the Sultan, he wanted to return right away with the wheat if they had given him. But the man before him smiled at him and said, "We have seen many men who came here to return but then settled; you'd better see our Sultan first!"

Yunus impatiently looked after the man who walked away with the thorn apples he picked. He didn't know how much time passed; the man who returned with a smile said, "Our Sultan would like you to have some rest and be our guest for three days, then he will make your wish come true," and showed Yunus a room where he could stay.

This made Yunus upset. He couldn't understand why he was waiting for three days.

In the evening, all guest gathered in the dining hall. They had dinner altogether and had some talk. Yunus was silently observing people in one corner. Why were all those people so peaceful and so happy? And what was the cause of that glow in their eyes? He was curious about that.

In the morning, he woke up in excitement. Three days had ended. He would see Sultan Hacı Bektash and return to his village. The same man came to him and asked him to perform ablution. He also explained Yunus how to act before the Sultan.

The door opened, and they entered in together. O Allah! Yunus had never seen such a beautiful man before. He was old, his hair and beard were snow-white, and he had a beautiful face. He could not understand the secret or the source of that beauty.

He kissed his hand and briefed the situation. The Sultan smiled at Yunus' impatience. He kept silent for some time, then asked: "Do you want breath or wheat?"

Yunus thought a little but he could not comprehend what the breath was. "My fellow villagers are starving. I want wheat, sir!" he answered.

The Sultan asked once more: "Alright, do you want breath equal to each thorn apple you brought or wheat?"

Yunus again silently said, "I want wheat, my fellow villagers are starving!" The Sultan asked again: "What if I give you breath equal to the seeds of the thorn apples?"

Yunus replied, "Sir, I don't know what breath is or what it is used for; I need wheat, the villagers looking forward to me." Hacı Bektash Wali understood that there was no point insisting and said, "Alright, son, let it be as you wish!"

Yunus got happy. He kissed the Sultan's hand and got out. The friendly man was no more smiling. It was as if his face discolored. He was upset for what Yunus missed and he was walking quietly. Yunus couldn't make sense of it either!

Once his cart was filled with wheat to its limit, Yunus bid farewell to everyone and set off. He had strange feelings inside. On one hand, he was happy that he would save his fellow villagers looking forward to him from starving; but on the other hand, he was strangely sad. He was sad for leaving that village, the place of peace and happiness.

What was breath? What did Hacı Bektash Wali want to give him insistently? What was it that he rejected? Should he first ask the Sultan to explain what breath was? Just as Yunus was thinking, suddenly a lightning stroke his heart. It was wisdom what the Sultan called breath; it was the truth, the resurrection. So, his heart was dead, and the Sultan wanted to resurrect it; he was offered immortality, but he insisted on wheat. As he continued thinking, he understood everything better. There was breath in that village; everyone was experiencing the comfort of finding what they had searched for. The cause of such abundance and happiness was breath.

He immediately turned his cart back. He quickly returned to the village of Hacı Bektash Wali. That friendly man was at the door waiting as if he had known that Yunus would come back. He got a twinkle in his eyes upon seeing Yunus, and he took him to the Sultan right away. He said, "He felt sorry and came back, sir!" But Hacı Bektash Wali said, "We offered the key to his heart to Tapduk Emre. He should go to him to get his breath; he is also one of us."

Hearing these words, Yunus couldn't decide whether to rejoice or sadden. But he had nothing left to do there. He now wanted to return to his village, deliver the wheat, and go to Sultan Tapduk.

When he arrived at the village, everyone welcomed him with delight. They unloaded the cart and shared the wheat. Everyone ate their fill, and now it was Yunus' turn. They asked Yunus about what he had seen and experienced, but Yunus kept his silence. He had an expression of regret on his face along with the happiness of having found the one to put up his fire inside. He declared just over there that he would leave to go to Tapduk Emre.

His mother felt so sad but there was nothing to do; it was not possible to hold Yunus there.

The other day, he set off early in the morning. He traveled day and night and reached Emre village. Similar to Bektash village, there was peace, happiness, abundance, and wealth in the village.

He appeared before Tapduk Emre. He submitted his body, spirit, soul, and life to Tapduk Emre, and threw himself at Tapduk Emre saying, "Give me breath, make me a man!"

Tapduk Emre assigned him to carry wood to the lodge. He went to the forest every morning after prayer, chopped wood until the evening call to prayer, and then, he returned to the lodge with the wood on his back. He was chopping wood, but such wood was that! He was working for hours to find straight wood thinking that crooked wood might not enter in his sheik's lodge. He only cared about Tapduk, he kept his nose clean, and he didn't pay attention to anyone. He only thought of properly fulfilling his duty and gaining the consent of his sheik.

One day, he was chopping wood in the forest. He chopped the straight ones as usual and piled them, but he couldn't find his rope to tie them. It was almost the time for evening call for prayer, and it was not possible to carry the wood to the lodge without the rope. He had never delayed his duty even for once throughout all those years, and he could not delay that day either; he could not return to the lodge empty handed. He was praying as he searched for his rope in panic when a thick black snake approached and twined around the wood. Yunus understood what had just happened, and thanked God. He held the black snake and took the wood on his back.

When the call for prayer started, Yunus entered in the lodge. He put the wood on the ground silently as he usually did. Then, understanding that his duty was over, the snake untwined and glided away. The disciples who saw that were amazed. They had already been jealous of Yunus for days. Tapduk's affection to Yunus, waiting for Yunus before starting the discourse, and Yunus' submission to Tapduk Sultan called everyone's attention. Some disciples who failed to be freed from the captivity of their egos; they were seeking ways to defame Yunus and were causing unrest.

No matter what they did, they failed to disgrace Yunus. Finally, one of them had an idea and claimed that Yunus' devotion to Tapduk was because of his love to Tapduk's daughter and, for that matter, Yunus had eye on Tapduk's place. Those words raised the devil.

Yunus was not aware of the things done behind his back; he continued his daily works as usual and he was busy chopping the finest wood for his sheik. One of those days, a couple of jealous disciples appeared before Tapduk and said, "Yunus laid his eyes on you daughter. He is following your daughter wherever she goes." Tapduk thought briefly and said, "So, go and beat him until he comes to his sense; then throw him out of the door!"

The disciples were happy to have their plan work; they caught and beat Yunus who was carrying wood unaware of anything. Then, they threw him in front of the door. Yunus could not understand what was going on and with a final effort he put his head on the sill. When the disciples closed the door, his head got stuck in between; yet, he said with a bitter smile: "Praise to God, I still have my head inside!"

Just then, a cry was heard. Tapduk Emre ran towards Yunus in tears saying, "Enough! Leave him, I finally found one!" The jealous disciples couldn't make sense out of it; they watched how Tapduk embraced Yunus and how he nestled his bleeding head in astonishment.

As the tears falling from his eyes were mixed with Yunus' blood, Tapduk Emre said, "You had been waiting for an opportunity. I allowed you for a moment and you almost crashed him. Leave him, He is mine! I won't hand over my Yunus to you, I may not spare my Yunus!" He picked Yunus up, took him into the lodge, and personally dressed his wounds.

As Yunus thought of what had happened, his heart ached, his whole body got numb and he was deeply hurt. What hurt Yunus was not the undeserved beating, his Sultan's sadness and crying because of him. He might have died to prevent his Sultan from frowning or shedding a single tear. He pondered long and found a solution at last.

He went to his Sultan headfirst and asked for permission. He explained that he might not stay there any longer, he didn't want to cause further unrest, and he couldn't stand Tapduk being upset. As he spoke, the flood of tears poured down his eyes but there were no other solutions. That was inevitable for his Tapduk to live in peace and safety.

The other morning, he set off in the wee hours. He hit the road without knowing where to go and without taking anything with him. He came up against two dervishes on the way. "Where are you heading, the wise men?" he asked. "We depend on the developments. We are heading wherever the road takes us!" they answered. Yunus asked: "May I join you?". When the dervishes accepted his offer, they continued to proceed together. After traveling for some time, they got hungry and one of those two dervishes opened his hand to pray. Upon his prayer, a table descended from above. Seeing that astonished Yunus, and he thought that his companions were of those loved by God. They sat together and ate their fill, then continued their way.

After covering a long distance, they got hungry again and this time, the other dervish prayed. Another table descended and they ate their meal in peace. When they got hungry for the third time, they told Yunus, "Come on dervish, it is your turn to pray now." Yunus didn't know what to do, and he couldn't persuade the dervishes even if he had told them that he couldn't do it. So, he raised his hands to the sky, and he prayed silently, "O my Lord! I am an incapable servant, please do not embarrass me. I am asking you for some food for the sake of the person who the dervishes mentioned in their prayers for food!" As soon as his prayer was over, not one but two tables descended from above. The dervishes were surprised, and asked, "O the humble dervish! We prayed and got one table, but you prayed and got two tables. What is the wisdom of this? For whose sake you asked for food from God?"

Yunus said, "First tell me whose name you mentioned while praying, and then I'll tell you." Dervishes explained, "We looked over the realm of meaning. We saw a man named Yunus who has a higher station and great value before God. So, we asked for food for his sake."

Upon hearing this, Yunus began to tremble from head to toe, and his heart ached thinking, "O my Tapduk, o my Sultan! What have you done to me? It seems that you made me so mature and made me ready without my knowledge!". When the dervishes asked, "Who did you mention in your prayer?" Yunus said, "Never mind, I am going back," and started to walk towards his Tapduk.

He walked day and night without sleeping or resting and reached the lodge of his Sultan. Tapduk's wife welcomed Yunus at the door. Yunus said, "Dear Haji Mother, please help me. Did my Tapduk forgive me? Can you ask him if he accepts me?" The old wife of Tapduk Emre responded, "Yunus, son, I love you very much. You are an honest, hardworking and a moral boy. I know that they treated you wrong, but my Tapduk got very upset after you. He couldn't stand the pain of losing you. He went blind of crying every day!"

Yunus regretted even further after hearing this. He understood better that he made a great mistake by leaving in order not to upset his Sultan. Yunus said, "Dear Haji Mother, please help me. Drive me back to my Tapduk!" by holding her hands tightly. Haji Mother said, "Alright, he will come out to perform ablution soon. He is walking with a stick as he cannot see. Lie on that door sill. When his stick catches you, he will ask me who you are. And I'll say, "This is Yunus," If he replies, "Which Yunus?" then leave silently. This means he still feels resentful. If he replies, "Is it our Yunus?" then embrace him and kiss his hand. This means he forgave you."

Yunus lied on the door sill and started waiting. Soon he heard the steps of Tapduk coming towards Yunus. Time was moving slowly for Yunus, and he was feeling himself at a place between heaven and hell.

As Haji Mother told, the stick caught Yunus. Tapduk asked:

"Dear, what is this on the floor?"

His wife replied, "It is Yunus." At that moment, Yunus could hear nothing but his heart beats. He felt like his heart skipped a beat.

When Tapduk asked, "Our Yunus?" Yunus Emre threw himself at the feet of his sheik and began to sob saying, "Forgive me, my Sultan, forgive me. I couldn't understand what you have given me!"

Tapduk said, "O Yunus! I prepared you as a closed box to offer our Lord as a gift without opening; but you hurried and opened the cover of the box. It may not be closed anymore. Now, speak whatever comes to your inner heart. You are in love; you are a lover of the Truth. You love everyone. You even love those who beat you to death. From now on, your duty is to love. Your mission is to be beneficial for the society. You will not have any enemies because you even love your enemies; so, no one can be angry at you," and thus, everyone recognized Yunus.

After that day, somethings happened to Yunus. The words fell into his heart in drops and he was speaking those words by astonishing everyone around. Each word he spoke burned another heart. His reputation spread from mouth to mouth and the number of people around him increased day by day. He felt uncomfortable about this; but he couldn't help speaking the words that came to his heart and he knew that the source of all those words was the Truth.

Yunus and Tapduk sometimes talked, sometimes shared their states, and sometimes just looked at each other in silence. They spent days like that. But one day, Tapduk called Yunus with eyes swollen of crying. A fireball fell in the heart of Yunus immediately. He knew that it was the fire of separation.

Tapduk said, "Come here, my Yunus. Come, the light of my eyes and my heart. I don't know how I may survive without your discourse and your friendly conversation, but there is one thing that I know very well. It is not possible for two lions to sit on one post. It is time for you to leave, the precious one of the Truth. Now go and serve. Tell Him and resurrect dead hearts with this breath that you took from us."

Upon hearing this, every particle of Yunus burnt with the fire of separation. Because he had learned what did it mean to be away from Tapduk; he had experienced that suffering before. How could he endure that pain once again? While he was crying with those thoughts, Tapduk Sultan held Yunus' hands and said, "Don't worry, we are now one. You are in me and I am in you. We became one with Him. We are not separating, praise be to God, we found unity in Him. Nobody can separate us from now on."

When Yunus heard those divine words, he gathered himself and comprehended the reality. He found solace in Tapduk's words.

That night, a farewell meeting was organized for Yunus. They performed dhikr, chanted hymns, and those who drank the wine of love got drunk.

Yunus woke up early in the morning and performed his morning prayer. He hit the road to go wherever his heart leads him without a certain destination.

On his way, he ran into saints form Khorasan. He asked, "Where are you going, dervishes?" They said, "Do you know Sultan Rumi? We are going to his lodge." Yunus had heard of Rumi many times but he couldn't find the chance to meet him. He took the opportunity and asked, "Can I join you?" When the dervishes accepted his offer, they proceeded together.

Dervishes were having a talk as they walked. But Yunus was not talking much; he became silent with the excitement of meeting Rumi and he became delighted with the divine light falling into his heart. He was briefly answering the questions asked and then returned to his silence again.

One of the dervishes wanted to eat semolina halva, and he called out to Rumi, "O my Sultan, we traveled long distances. We are hungry. Could you please offer us a nice and tasty halva?" The others also wanted some and confirmed altogether. Yunus was silent again.

Finally, they reached Konya. Then, they found Rumi's lodge. As soon as they entered in, they smelled the sweat odor of halva, and smiled each other saying, "The Sultan heard us!"

Rumi welcomed them standing. He embraced them one by one and smelled each one as if he was looking for a particular person, but he couldn't. He talked to all dervishes and none left behind. Then, he asked: "You asked for halva and I got it prepared. One of you asked for my essence, my truth but where is he? I cannot see him?"

Just then, they remembered Yunus. "Where did that humble man hide? We entered in together," murmured the dervishes. Suddenly, Rumi noticed someone behind the door sitting on heels. He couldn't tell he was there, and he was the one asking for him out of decency, and he was sitting there silently in tears.

Seeing Yunus, Rumi said with a groan: "O my dear!" He made quick steps towards that dervish who flamed the fire of longing in his heart. At that moment, Yunus also proceeded towards Rumi with an irresistible attraction and they met in the middle. They embraced and lost themselves.

Rumi didn't let Yunus get out of his sight throughout his stay in Konya. Rumi tried to fulfill his longing to Shams with Yunus. They frequently performed seclusion, and they exchanged from their hearts for days.

People of Konya started to surge up once again. Did a new Shams arrive? They could not see Rumi for days.

What was it about that humble dervish that they shut themselves and did not come out for days. But there was one thing that they didn't know. Yunus was the Turkmen dervish for whom Rumi said, "In every divine destination that I ascended, I saw the footprints of a great Turkmen man before me." Rumi called Husam Al-Din Chalabi and asked him to read Mathnawi to Yunus. Husam Al-Din Chalabi read each and every page of Mathnawi. And Yunus listened to him. Then, with eyes looking from another realm and with a voice from an unclear direction, he said, "I disguised myself in flesh and bones, presented myself as Yunus." Hearing that, Rumi smiled and quiet Husam Al-Din Chalabi down. "We explained it with too many words, my Husam Al-Din. See, Yunus briefed it with one sentence," he said. Yunus startled at that moment and gathered himself; he looked at Rumi's face bashfully thinking that he might have done something wrong. But he could only see pleasure in Rumi's face.

While Yunus and Rumi continued fulfilling their longing, the people were surging up with anger. Yunus was aware of what was happening, and one day, he asked permission to leave. He said, "It is time to go." Although Rumi insisted saying, "Don't go, you have salved me. Let's spend our days together from now on," Yunus said, "I was told to travel and tell. I should continue until I am told to stop. It is not good for me to stay for a long time in one place," and took leave.

Throughout his life, Yunus never claimed to be a dervish or wanted to become a sultan; he abandoned existence and attained the happiness of nothingness; he became the source of hope for sufferer and he traveled Anatolia, Syria, and Azerbaijan.

There are many disputes about the places of birth and burial of Yunus Emre. It is apparent that he was born in the center of Anatolia and buried in the hearts of his lovers. Therefore, he has tombs in many cities and provinces. Let's consider that all of them are true and visit him everywhere he has a tomb. Because Yunus is everywhere he is remembered.

MOURNFUL YUNUS

"As a person, Yunus Emre is mournful, humble, and a lover."

The sadness of Yunus originates from the observations he made at an early age and his becoming aware of the source of such a heavy burden of living.

This awareness allowed him to observe the happenings in life at a higher level first beyond his village, then the cities and countries; he observed what made people suffer from, he resolved their problems by finding solutions from his perspective, and he reflected the results in his poems with plain language.

Yunus first addressed the causes of sufferings, then analyzed their effects on people, and comprehended that most of them are beneficial factors that mature people. He saw how different suffering people were from others. In other words, he determined the fact that the remedy of the people was hidden in their sufferings.

It is understood from here that people with problems think, people with problems seek remedies, and they apprehend the truth of life while searching!

They help the others who suffer; they show the beneficial outcomes of sufferings; and they prevent others from cursing and falling. Sufferings are like remedies; they taste bitter, but they cure. So, in this sense, many poems of Yunus have been a prescription for the entire humanity.

HUMBLE YUNUS

Finally, the mourning Yunus was drawn into a whirlpool of a greater suffering which was the loneliness caused by being separated from the Truth; he became a humble man of Truth who suffers from being alone in crowds.

Humble Yunus traveled from one city to another and crossed the mountains but he couldn't find anyone with teary eyes and wounded heart like him. He burned out with longing day and night, his mouth spoke, and his eyes shed tears, but he still couldn't meet his lover. He separated from the true friend to come to this world. He got tired of the distress of this world. He wanted to go to the true friend by breaking the chains attaching him to this world. If he had born hundred thousand times, he would still have wanted to sacrifice himself for the sake of the true friend. He mentioned that he had come to a strange land, nobody understood him, and he had a dialog of the deaf; and he emphasized that people failed to see the reality. He defined himself as a nightingale in the garden of the Beloved, and the Beloved as his unfading, everlasting rose. By mentioning that the Beloved called him and gave him a glass of wine of love, he declared that he attained the secret of immortality after drinking from that wine.

LOVER YUNUS

In Sufism, divine love is the most important aspect on the path of becoming a perfect man. Divine love is the glorified version of love of God. And the love that Yunus repeatedly mentioned is this love. Besides being an important aspect in Sufism, divine love has a significant place in the poems and the personality of Yunus Emre. According to masters of Sufism, divine love, of which Yunus represents one of the best examples in his personality, occurs when the Almighty Creator presents Himself to Himself in form of a lover and a beloved to observe the glories of His names and attributes.

Yunus loved the mountains and rocks. He loved the trees and birds. He loved the Beloved of all. He got sick with longing. He traveled many lands. He sought the Beloved. He asked about Him to ants and the flying birds. He asked about Him to sufferers and the poor, but he couldn't find. He burned out with this live throughout his life. Finally, he found the Beloved of all. He scattered his ashes on the ocean.

HIS WORKS

Yunus Emre based his works on love and tolerance. He is one of the masters of Sufism who explained and taught these two topics to people in the most effective manner.

Yunus Emre has two works which are his Divan and his mathnawi, Risalatun Nushiyye.

All his poems are compiled in his divan. He is sincere, pure, and clear. He stayed away from showing off and embellishments in his poems. His expressions are considerably effective and strong, but he used a plain Turkish. He made great services to Turkish culture by choosing Turkish language. He is one of those who paved the way for folk literature in Anatolia and who played the biggest role in this.

Yunus considered poems as a means. His poems are didactic and realistic. Although he didn't have artistic concerns in his poems, he addressed people in the best way and produced great artistic works. He speaks to everyone in every segment of society including the high-level intellectual people, and his messages reach their targets. He hit the roads, visited cities and villages, and explained the truth to people he ran into.

Yunus didn't care about the social statuses of the people he addressed, and he didn't distinguish them based on their religion, order, race, or color. He never discriminated anyone. He had an attitude that embraces the whole humankind. He was not a separatist, but a unifier and a joiner. He explained Sufism down to the very last detailed in his poems, and his plain language made it easier for people to reach the truth. In his work in form of mathnawi, Risaletun Nushiyye, Yunus Emre explained the reason of creation and the good and bad tempers with symbols.

CHAPTER TWO

PERSPECTIVE OF YUNUS EMRE

PRESENTATION

O the mankind! Stop and think! Why and what for was Adam created?

What is the essence, the reality of the worldly life?

Does death mean vanishing off the face of the earth? Or does your spirit abandon the body and born into a new life?

What is the true purpose of the worships? Why do we perform prayer or

why do we fast?

Do you know your Lord? You may not know Him before you know yourself.

Then, how can one know himself?

How is the self-disciplined and the soul purified?

Everything has a truth. Knowing the reality of the truths is possible by finding the Truth.

Look, how Yunus Emre found:

I found the Truth by reaching the saint
I saw the beauty of the Truth by seeing the face of the saint

This is the password.

Marifa (gnosis) is the ability to know the Truth. How does Marifa (gnosis) achieved? What did the friends of God who are experts of Marifa (gnosis) experience and what did they say?

We have prepared the detailed answers to all these questions for those who seek for the truth.

How happy are those good servants who found Him; who live or who spend their lives with a desire to live the reality by hearing with Him and seeing with Him as experts of marifa (gnosis) on the path of truth!

HIDDEN TREASURE

Our Almighty Creator was a hidden treasure in the past eternity; He wanted to be known and He created the universe, which is the realm of all creatures, and the mankind.

He created this great universe to exhibit His names and attributes which constitute the magnificent treasure.

From the atoms to billions of galaxies containing billions of stars, the entire universe undertook this duty to exhibit His treasure.

There are hundreds of billions of galaxies in the universe, and there are hundreds of billions of stars in each galaxy. It is mentioned that the largest galaxies contain three trillion stars. Let's think of the power created such a great universe, so that we could have some knowledge about His unlimited might. Let's also analyze the custom galaxy images; let's witness that great design technique and be impressed by all these seeing the beautiful images from billions of galaxies containing billions of stars.

Our galaxy is named the Milky Way and the Solar System is within this galaxy.

These galaxies are pivoting around a center with its hundreds of billions of stars.

What kind of a power is it that turns the billions of galaxies together with their hundreds of billions of stars? Such a great order, such a great organization is this? How can we underrate such an enormous system by calling it a coincidence?

Our Almighty Creator wanted to be known by exhibiting His names and attributes through all the creatures in such an enormous universe. He endowed the creatures with the ability to display His treasure. He placed a pearl into the secret of each property from His treasure.

He created the plurality of the realm of creation out of the oneness of His essence, and He furnished them with pearls and jewelries. Then, He created man, the most dignified of all the creation, to be known.

He saw and examined the realm of creation by being the hearing ears and the seeing eyes of a purified man.

He watched the oneness in His essence on the plurality in the creation through the eyes of the man He created. He made His treasure on again by having man to gather His names and attributes one by one, and He entitled man to represent Him. He said, "One who sees you is like he has seen Me!" He encouraged other men to see that purified and matured perfect man.

This is the "perfect man" who is the successor or our Almighty Creator. One who sees him is like he has seen God.

The abundance of the names and attributes of our Almighty Creator gather and manifest on his face and display the beauty of the Truth.

The hidden treasure is the Truth, and it is real. We came to this world to find Him and to see Him.

He may not be known before one is purified and loses himself.

Only He may see Him. Only He may know Him.

He was a hidden treasure, He wanted to watch Himself and He created the universe, the realm of creation, as a divine mirror. He looked at Him through the eyes of a man whose heart He entered in. Because He wouldn't have fit into the universe.

That hidden treasure, which is the realm of creation and which garnishes the universe with its jewelries, shaped in flesh and bones, disguised in Yunus Emre, and called out through Mansoor, "Ana al-Haqq!" He said, "I am the Truth!"

That's why our Prophet said, "The one who sees me is like he has seen the Truth; love me more than yourselves!" He is the most beautiful example of the purified men, and he is the representative of the Truth. We must profoundly love him to attain the purpose of living, and we should attain the ability to love our Creator like him.

Only those who love Him like our Prophet may find Him.

Look, do you see? How may not you see the light when there is light. It is hidden with its oneness, but it is apparent with its attributes, its colors, on all the creatures. We cannot see it although it is clearly apparent. But every color that we see on the creatures is the light, isn't it? Every creature that we look at shows us the light, doesn't it? Although the colors belong to the light, we suppose that they belong to the creatures.

When we gather all the colors in a wheel and turn it, the colors show the light; and just like this, the whirling of a mature man who gathered the beautiful attributes of God in himself shows us the manifestation of the Truth.

Man is created to find the hidden treasure. That hidden treasure is the Truth, it is the reality. The one who does not seek Him lives in vain. The Almighty Creator achieves the purpose of creation in the man who finds Him. He honors and glorifies that man with Himself.

All the creation is mortal, and only God is eternal. He is evident in the universe with His attributes and hidden with His essence. He has covered all the creatures with His knowledge. Only He knows His essence.

He hears, He is the All-Hearing; He sees, He is the All-Seeing. He doesn't need anyone.

. He is self-sufficient and rich.

God exists with His essence. Yet, the creatures exist with Him. There is no existence other than God.

When God loves one of His servants, He makes that servant fall in love with Him. That servant properly follows the commands of God. He is equipped with beautiful attributes and adopts good moral. The secret of the angelic realm is revealed to such a man, and he sees the spirits of the Prophets with their subtle bodies. He observes the realm of spirits.

God did not fit into the earth and the sky, but He fit into the heart of a true believer. Let's cleanse our hearts from everything other than the Truth, so that the manifestation of the Truth fills into those hearts.

The believers say, "There is no god, but God!" The wise men say, "There is no one, but God!"

He is the Truth; He is the hidden treasure.

The reality of His absolute existence covers the whole that is referred as the Truth and the creation.

It is Him who shows His beauty through His attributes. Knowledge may not identify Him. The bodily eyes may not see Him. He is the First and the Last.

He lives the life in a complete manner.

He is the origin of everything with His name al-Qadir (the All Powerful).

He is one and only with His essence. There is nothing that constitutes Him. He does not have a partner or a friend.

Nothing can move or stop without His might and will.

It is Him who is apparent by manifesting in every perfection with the Truth. It is Him who displays His oneness in all pluralities through unity.

It is Him who expresses the greatness of His essence through His excellence and honoring. He may not be described or compared. Mind may not reach Him. Scholars may not comprehend Him. He is the light of faith and comprehension.

He knows the past and the future.

There is no deity! There is only Him, the one and only God. Hazrat Muhammed is His servant and His messenger. He is the place of manifestation and mirror of God's essence.

He talks to His servants by giving inspirations to their hearts. He sends manifestations of His essence and His attributes to the hearts of His servants.

If He becomes the eyes and the ears of His beloved servant, nothing remains as secret to that servant.

He created man based on His image, He named man with His beautiful names and furnished Him with His qualities. Therefore:

He is al-Hayy, the Living; so, you live, too. He is al-Alim, the Knower; so, you know, too.

He is as-Sami, the All-Hearing; so, you hear, too. He is al-Basir, the All-Seeing; so, you see, too.

The wine of His reality pours out from the mouth of the one giving a discourse and it takes those who drink that wine by listening to the realm of secrets. However, when some people become sober, they deny the taste of that wine and become depraved.

O the one seeking the hidden treasure! Remember, the reality is hidden in a mirror. The reality is not separate from the mirror from which it is seen.

The one seeking the reality first sees the Truth in His beautiful names and attributes. Then he watches His essence in his heart.

That hidden treasure is hidden in objects with His name "concealed." He is seen with His name "apparent."

The one who tells about Him may not tell the reality unless he loses himself as he talks. The Truth tells Himself with the one who loses himself. God is known through His names and attributes. The Truth may only be reached through His names and attributes. The name "Allah (God)" covers all names and attributes. In this sense, the name Allah has become a mirror for man. If one looks into this mirror, he understands the meaning of "Allah exists, and there is nothing except for Him!" He discovers that his hearing is the hearing of Allah; his seeing is the seeing of Allah; his talking is the talking of Allah; his knowledge is the knowledge of Allah; his will is the will of Allah; his power is the power of Allah; his life is the life of Allah, and

he knows that his capabilities actually belong to Allah.

The Almighty God says in His Scripture, "Allah created you and whatever you do!" (Surah As-Saffat, Verse 96).

When a servant performs an action, he performs that action through the will and power of Allah. Allah actually performs that action; however, anything that is good and nice is from Allah, but those wrong and improper are from our ego.

A Sufi expressed as follows in one of his poems: Look, the waves of God's sea brought a pearl to the shore with the storm. Look at that pearl, take of your garment, jump into that sea, and surrender yourself. You no more need to take out a pearl by relying on your ability to swim. Now, you die in that sea and let your life become God's life; because only the dead are comfortable in that sea.

The name "Allah" existed when there were no words. This name does not derive from any word. The universe rotates with His appeal by glorifying this name.

The first letter (alif) of the name "Allah" refers to His unity, namely His oneness; the second letter (lam) refers to His majesty; the third letter (the second lam) to His beauty; the fourth letter (hidden alif) to His perfection; and the fifth letter (ha) refers to the creation.

In this sense, the Almighty Allah says, "Allah is the protector!" (Surah ash-Shura, verse 9).

Man is also a protector. In other words, being a protector is the identity of the Truth and manifests in man.

The Almighty Allah first created the intellect. Then He created the soul, the light, the pen, the slate, the throne, the stool, the heaven, the hell, the angels and jinns, the earth and the sky, and the stars, respectively.

After all these, Allah said to the angels, "I will create a successor on the earth!" and He created Adam.

The angels replied, "O Lord, will you create a man who will be in mischief and shed blood? But we glorify and extol You..." Allah ordered, "Indeed, I know what you don't know!"

Thereupon, the angels were scared of the greatness of Allah and circumambulated the throne seven times. Thus, it became necessary to circumambulate the Kaaba seven times.

CREATION OF HAZRAT ADAM

Yunus Emre explains the creation of Hazrat Adam, the first man, as follows:

Allah mixed the soil and water and made a mud. He shaped this mud in form of a man. This shaped mud was dried with air. Then, it was superheated with fire. This heating process led to rigidity and durability.

Finally, Allah gave life to Adam's body by blowing a soul from His soul.

Just then, Adam, who became alive, looked at the sky and saw the writing, "There is no god but Allah, and Muhammed is His messenger!" and asked the Almighty Creator about this. He said, "O Lord! Whose name is this that You mention with Your name?" His Creator explained him that it was Hazrat Muhammed Mustafa. He told that He created Adam from his light. He stated that he would be descended on the earth as the final prophet and that he would physically be the son of Adam.

The soul entered in Adam's body and filled him with light. The body loved the soul and welcomed it. The body embraced the soul. It praised and thanked.

This first man created received the following attributes from soil: Patience, good manner, trust (entrusting everything to Allah), being content with destiny, reliance, and dignity.

Water brought four attributes. These are purity (cleanness), generosity, grace (charity and beneficence) and joining. Man acquired the ability to clean, to have wealth, to be generous, to do good, to carry and to join from water.

Air brought four whims to man. Air is whim. These are faction (lie), hypocrisy, quickness (precipitance, impatience) and egocentric worldly desires. Air impacted man negatively. It caused man to form bad habits compared to water and soil.

Fire brought the following tastes and joys to man which lead to negations like air: Lust, egocentric desires, arrogance, greed, and jealousy. These are the negative desires deriving from the physical nature of man.

These explanations are very important for us to know man.

Soil was created from the light of Allah. Water is from Allah's light of life, and it gives life. Wind is from the grandeur of Allah, and it gives grandeur. Fire is from the rage of Allah, and it burns. Allah mollifies His anger with fire. Soil and water belong to heaven while fire and wind belong to hell. The one who depends on soil and water enters the heaven; the one who depends on fire and wind enters the hell.

Apart from the physical being, man also has attributes from his soul. The first one of these attributed is dignity, honor, and nobility. As we know, Allah created man as the most dignified of all creatures. This dignity derives from man's soul. The second one is unity and oneness. The power to reach oneness from contradictions and to reach Allah from oneness is unity. It is the ability to join Allah by acting with a feeling of unity and solidarity. The third one is modesty, sense of shame. The indication of this is blushing. If there is no modesty left in a society, the morals immediately collapse in that society. The sense of shame prevents improper actions of the society. The last one is decency. We may walk toward our Creator in decency. Allah would not allow an indecent man to appear in His presence. Allah fondly accepts His servant who turns toward Him timidly, sadly, and shyly.

Although Allah had the angels build the body of Adam He made his face with His hand of power. This is why our Prophet said, "Do not hit one on the face!" Hitting on the face has two meanings: The first one is to slap someone in the face; and the other is to hold something against someone.

Looking at the face of mature men is very impressive. Allah didn't create anything ugly. All faces are beautiful. The subsequent impairments have arisen from the wrong living of the ancestors. For example, if one catches syphilis, the generations after him would become ugly.

There are three types of intellect:

The first one is the intellect for subsistence which is used to work and earn money, and which apprehends the world order. This is the type of intellect that is dominant in most of the people.

The second one is the intellect for the afterlife. This is the intellect that comprehends the states of the afterlife. This is the intellect that makes research and discoveries about the afterlife, and it dives into the realm of secret.

The third one is the intellect that understands and notifies about the gnosis of Allah. This is called the universal intellect (aql al-kulli).

The Almighty Allah gathered all the angels and commanded them to prostrate Adam. Although all angels obeyed this command, the devil acted arrogantly and refused to prostrate. He became one of the rebels. Then, Allah placed Adam into the heaven. Adam's heart failed to find peace in the heaven. Thereupon, Allah made Adam sleep. He created Eve from the left rib of Adam. When Adam woke up, he saw Eve beside him. Thus, Adam's heart found peace with Eve.

Allah said to them, "Live in my heaven. Eat from these fruits but stay away from this tree. May my greetings and mercy be upon you..."

The devil envied this dignity and honoring to Adam by Allah. He wanted to take him out of the heaven. He came to the door of the heaven by disguising himself as a snake. He began crying there. Adam and Eve didn't recognize him. They asked why he was crying. He said:

"I am crying for you. Because some time later you will be separated, and you will be longing for each other. If you eat the fruit of that tree, you stay in the heaven forever..." Thereupon, Eve said to Adam:

"Come on, let's eat the fruit of that tree and stay in the heaven forever..." Adam replied:

"The Almighty Allah forbid eating from that tree!"

Eve insisted:

"Please, let's eat if you love me, so that we stay in the heaven forever!" Believing in the words of the devil, Eve picked and ate some fruit from the tree and said "Allah's grace is abundant..."

She picked another fruit and gave it to Adam. As soon as they bite that fruit, all their clothes disappeared. They got totally naked. They ran and hid with shame. They picked leaves from the fig tree and covered themselves.

In consequence, Allah took them out of His heaven and descended them on the earth. He placed them apart from each other. And He allowed the devil to harass the human race.

WORLDLY LIFE

This world will also end one day. The day of judgment will come, and all the creatures will die out.

The signs of this are clearly seen today:

The ozone layer of the atmosphere is punctured. The harmful rays of the sun cannot be filtered. Diseases, cancers increased.

The ice on the poles is swiftly melting and turning into water! Where will all the water go eventually? There will be no land left on the earth. Where will the people live?

Inside the earth is filled with lava, the fire is burning. The volcanoes acting as a chimney to relieve the earth by releasing the lava and gases are getting clogged one by one. What will happen if the earth is not relieved by releasing the high energy inside it?

The cool soil layer holding the earth is at the rate of the orange peel to the fruit. For how long the earth will hold this energy inside? Even the idea of cracking and breaking of that cluster is fearful!

The end of the world will come like this or in another unexpected way; when and how will be the end of the world? Our Almighty Creator knows this. It will arrive when the time He has given ends. The earth has a certain lifetime just like every creation.

Actually, the worldly life is nothing. There is death at the end. When we die, this worldly life also ends.

Let's wake up!

Do not get lost in the temporary pleasures of this world. Let's live as aware, let's see the truths. Let's join the group of wise servants and live a life compliant to the purpose of creation. Remember, we were created to know our Creator. The true life starts only after knowing Him. Those who live without knowing Him only serve to their bodies and live their lives in vain assuming that this is how life shout be.

The worldly life is the enemy of people. It takes them away from Allah. Do not get lost in the charm of the world. No matter what we eat, drink or experience, our body will decay and be mixed up in soil. Let's wake up my friends, the time passes quickly. Our childhood is just like yesterday... Today, we have wrinkles on our face and gray hair; the life is abandoning us.

Yunus Emre likens the world to a witch. It adorns itself and looks charming to people; it attaches people to itself and consumes their lives. When they get old, it turns its back to them and leaves them. In this sense, the worldly life is an unfaithful and disloyal lover. It throws away the eternal future of a man.

Do not set your heart on worldly pleasures, or you will fall into world's trap one day. This world is an absorber and absorbs even the wise men, it will also absorb us when death arrives one day See the reality, my brother, many passed away and mixed up in soil, it will also take us into its arms one day if it is ready to fly like a falcon, like an arrow released from its bow, it will fly to the Truth one day.

Poor Yunus never claim that you have seen and learned, Hold on to the saints and flow like the streams one day.
– *Yunus Emre*

This does not mean that we will not work or acquire any property in this world. Quite the contrary, we will work hard and earn much. We will do charity and serve with what we earn. In other words, we will earn for the sake of Allah in this world and spend it for the sake of Allah. We will not fill in our hearts with worldly desires and wishes or become a slave to the world.

In the end, we will stay away from the worldly life that causes us to forget Allah. Because the place of those who lose themselves in the world would be the hell in the afterlife.

When people see the reality after dying, they would think:

"Oh, my Lord! Please return me to the life on earth. I hope I do good deeds in that which I have left behind." (Surah Muminun, verses 99-100)

Those who spend this worldly life being negligent from Allah and who make an illegal fortune without considering what is permitted or forbidden would only understand after they die that love for the world detract them from Allah. But unfortunately, there is no turning back. It's no-good crying over spilled milk. May Allah protect us from being a penitent!

Let's wake up when we still have the opportunity. Let's turn our hearts toward Allah and know Him by fulfilling His requests. Let's live a beautiful life and return to our origin.

From another point of view, this world is like a marketplace. Let's work and

earn in the way it is permitted. Let's do charity for the sake of Allah. Let's never forget our Master. Let's appear before the Truth at the end with the good deeds we gained from this world.

As long as we live in the world, let us offer to others from the subsistence given to us by Allah.

Let's help the needy and the poor. Let's regard their needs as more important than ours.

To that effect, our Prophet said:

"Whoever fulfills a need of a Muslim brother or sister, Allah fulfills seventy needs of him on the day of judgment."

Let us abandon the world before it leaves us. Let's build our grave before we lie in it. Let's make our Lord content of ourselves before meeting Him.

Our Prophet said, "The world is the seeding field of the afterlife…" What goes around in this world comes around in the afterlife.

Again, like our Prophet said: "Let's work as if we will never die, and let's worship as if we will die tomorrow."

Let's be grateful for the blessings bestowed upon us by Allah. Let's express our gratitude a lot. Unfortunately, we are not expressing our gratitude. We think that we worked, and we gained. How did we earn? We earned with a sound mind and a healthy body. We don't know who gave this health to us! Moreover, who gave ourselves to us! We didn't exist in the past; we don't think about who allowed us to exist! We do not consider this. We came to the world, we grew old, we got lost in daily works, and we are leaving. Such a negligence? We will account for what we possess. There is a detailed balance sheet, a statement of profit and loss for how we use our possessions.

Tomorrow in the afterlife, even if we deny the sins we commit in this world, our organs will testify; our hands will admit that they took, our eyes will admit that they have looked, our ears will admit that they heard, and our mouth will admit that it has eaten.

Allah stated this as follows:

"Their ears, their eyes, and their skins shall bear witness against them." (Surah Fussilat, Verse 20)

Think of all those who passed by this world. The rich, the sultans, the brave men, all handed over their bodies to the mother earth. They didn't take anything from the world but their good and bad deeds. They worked hard and saved. At the end, they left it all behind.

It is good to remember this saying of our Prophet: "Whoever only loves his worldly life will suffer in his afterlife.

Whoever only loves his afterlife will suffer in his worldly life." "Those who seek for the friendship of Allah would neither be satisfied with this world nor the

afterlife."

No matter how much worldly wealth we have, there is no harm in being rich as long as we do not set our hearts on our wealth, and we do charity out of it.

Some prophets were also very rich; but they did a lot of charities like Solomon.

Work for this world but avoid losing your heart to the world. Those who lose their hearts to the world may be easily deceived by the delusions of the devil. Remember Allah. Work for the sake of Allah.

Visit a cemetery and check what is written on the headstones. The governors, the sultans are lying in there. Newborn babies were placed into the graves before they even learned to crawl.

Think that you will also go there tomorrow.

Days, months, years are passing quickly.

Who does the houses, lands, vineyards, and orchards that we possess in this world belong to; to whom these will be left? What did Yunus Emre say: "Goods and chattels, both are lies Go ahead, linger over for some time." The best is to abandon this world before dying. In other words, let's take it out of our hearts. Only then we join the Truth, and we reach the eternity with the Truth.

When Abraham Edhem understood the reality, he renounced his throne, became a dervish to find the Truth and lived a different life.

In the afterlife, people assume that they lived in the world for one or two days. It feels that short. Just like the dreams that we see for a couple of seconds during sleep but last for years.

No matter how rich, how high-ranking, or how authorized you are in this world, never patronize anyone or become arrogant! One day you will also become powerless. You may no longer stand up and you take leave from the world. Your body decays and perishes in the soil.

O my poor brothers and sisters, what do we have to boast about?

Was it you who created the world that you step on earth with pride, you underestimate people and regard with dislike?

Can you embrace the dead body of the person you love the most this life? How much more you can love and for how long you can stay with him or her? When the body starts to decay and smell, we look for a place to hide. So, this is the reality. Death has arrived to them today, and it will arrive to us tomorrow.

What do we have to boast around this much? Let's think of the origin of our body. Let's remember where we came from and be humble.

Do not hurt anyone. It is very dangerous to break a heart.

Particularly, a heart that has Allah in it.

Do not be reckless. Show courtesy to people. Speak prudently. Do not talk in vain. When appropriate, you lay claim on all good virtues and tell that you always do good deeds. You want to make others believe in what you tell. This is not correct.

Let's stop admiring ourselves and putting on makeup and ask others what kind of a person we are and how we influence our circle.

Because the bad-tempered people also talk about themselves as a good person. They immediately forget about the evil they do.

Do not brag on or expect to be praised for how nice you treat people. Think that you only do it for the sake of Allah and do not make an effort to receive the favor of the public, but the Truth. Above all, do not constantly remind anyone the favor you do. Or you lose the merit for that favor.

Allah declares this as follows: "O you who believe! cancel not your charity by reminders of your generosity or by injury." (Surah al-Baqarah, verse 264)

You say, "He will die, she will die!" but why you do not say, "I will also die one day!" Put your hand on your head and move it around. What is the difference between your head and the skulls in the graves? Consider all these facts, and do not hurt anyone, do not break hearts, or do not deceive anyone.

Let's turn our hearts toward Allah as long as we live in the world. Do not turn away from Him.

In this respect, the Almighty Allah says:

O you who believe, let not your wealth and your children divert you from the remembrance of Allah. And whoever does that - then those are the losers." (Surah al-Munafiqun, Verse 9)

Hearts blacken with the love of world and lighten with the love of Allah.

Remember Allah in everything we do and in every state we are in; forgetting about Allah is a disaster! If a servant forgets about Allah, then Allah forgets about His servant. Try to say "ALLAH!" by addressing Him in the way He asked. If a person says "ALLAH!" for once with his tongue, his heart and all his organs, all his wishes come true. But he still wishes Allah.

Allah warns us:

"They forgot Allah, and Allah also forgot them." (Surah at-Tawba, verse 67)

Properties and wealth acquired with legal (halal) earnings are propitious unless you forget Allah by thinking too much about your properties and as long as you use your properties in good deeds.

You should fill the hungry, dress the unclothed, help those in debt, and build charitable institutions like mosques, schools, and hospitals.

You need to spend the fortune given by Allah for the sake of Allah. You should not just save up for a lifetime.

You may be a man of property; we may work hard and earn; what matters is to keep these properties away from your heart. There is no objection to this as long as you do not put them into your heart. If you put them into your heart, the property leads to unrest. You become a slave of endless wishes and desires thinking to buy something all the time. We are not satisfied with less. We are not content with what you find. We are blaming Allah claiming that He did not give you what you want although you asked for and begged Him many times and you worshiped a lot. Have you ever thought how would be the end of this life? When will all these wishes end?

The pharaoh who relied on the abundance of his properties declared his deity in the end. Today, the faith of those who rely on their properties weakens.

Spend from the properties and wealth you earned legitimately for the sake of Allah; be generous. Generosity is from the Most Compassionate (ar-Rahman); stinginess is from the devil.

When you want to use your properties and wealth for the sake of Allah, the devil deludes you. The devil frightens you, saying, "Do not spend from your wealth, or you will be down and become needy!"

Our Prophet said, "A stingy may not enter the heaven even if he is a devotee!"

Stinginess is one of the worst qualities. Whatever you have of this quality, you need to abandon it as soon as possible. Then, you may be a servant worthy of Allah and His messenger. Generous people enter the heaven first. Regarding generosity and stinginess, Allah says:

"Whoever comes with a good deed will be rewarded tenfold." (Surah al-Anam, verse 160)

"Whatever you spend in charity, Allah will compensate you for it." (Surah Saba, Verse 39)

We leave this world not with what we collected, but what we distributed. So, do charitable deeds as much as possible. Find the true poor people; search for those who do not beg people; ask help of Allah to recognize them. Be a "CHASER of POOR." Please a poor man with a single move, hear him saying, "MAY ALLAH BE PLEASED WITH YOU!" and disappear.

DEATH

A single cell is formed with the combination of two cells of a married couple, and this cell divides to produce cells and within a period of four months, they form a small body inside the mother's womb. In the meantime, Allah blows a spirit into this body and revives it. During the subsequent five months, the spirit accommodates itself to the body, takes the body under its control, and comes into this world by leaving the mother's womb.

In terms of the spirit, this is to enter into the grave, while, in terms of the body, this is to be born into this world.

Afterwards, the body of the newborn baby grows and

Develops, and starts living by adopting the worldly life with its spirit.

The young and healthy body wears out in time, it gets sick and becomes older.

The spirit, pleased with itself in this mobile grave of body, is disturbed by the pain and discomfort, and it immediately wants to leave the body.

Finally, the lifesaver angel called Azrael comes and pulls the spirit out of the body cage where it has been captive for years.

This event is death to body, but salvation to spirit. What we call death is the death of the body. It is the body which decays and gets mixed up with soil. However, bodies of certain people do not decay even if they remain in soil for years. There are many examples of this in our country. There is another reason for this.

Abandon your concerns about death, the lovers won't die, they are eternal. Death is the breath of the lover, because it is the divine light for reunion. Don't be afraid of death, it takes you to the Truth. Death takes you to eternity, fear of death is a mischief.

Look at this ore, the hidden treasure, the light. How may this light disappear, the Creator views it. In the realm of spirits, we were together before our Lord asks Understand the origin of this servant.

We used to know each other and attained the unity in the past. We entered in the body and fell apart like all creatures. We are no strangers due to the Creator if you are aware. The path of ultimate reunion is the strongest path if you seek and follow.

He has authority on His property, He knows what to do. The truth is that this property is home to His existence Good news Yunus, they ask you to come to the true friend. This is an invitation by the One saying, "Everything shall return to Him!"

– *Yunus Emre*

What a person calls me is not the body, but the spirit. Therefore, people do not die. The body, which is the mount, dies.

All cells in the body die and renewed at a certain period. So, a person's body dies and revives many times during the lifetime. This happens with the attachment of body to the spirit. When the spirit leaves the body, the body impairs, decays, and dies. In other words, life comes to body through the spirit. Body revives with the spirit. The body without the spirit is corpse. The cells of your current body are not the same as the cells of your body as a child. While to body is constantly renewed, the spirit remains the same. The spirit does not die or decay. Because the spirit is made of the angelic ore.

At the following stage, the worldly life ends, and the afterlife begins.

Do not wait for the Judgment Day to come. One's death is his Judgment Day. There is no certain time of death for anyone; so, make the necessary preparations for the afterlife. Everyone revives in the afterlife the way they die.

Regarding this matter, our Prophet said:

"You die the way live; you are revived the way you die."

Remember your relatives who passed away before you. You will die just like they did. Do not think that anyone will stay in this world forever. Death is the truth. Every ego will taste death. If you pay attention, the word "taste" refers that death is sweet or bitter. May Allah predestine us a sweet death. Do not forget death, remember it all the time. It is a very important advice.

THE AFTERLIFE

This is the eternal life to start after the worldly life.

People migrate to the afterlife after living in the world for a certain time. They are rewarded or punished there based on their deeds in the world.

Those who obey the commands of the Almighty Creator and live as He wishes are rewarded with the heaven; however, those who rebel, disobey the commands and sin are punished with the hell.

While there is a lot of grace and blessings in the heaven, the hell is full of fire and it burns down the sins. Once the sinners burn down and serve their sentences for some time in the hell, they get washed in the stream called "Life," and they are sent to the heaven where they will stay forever with other people.

Remember the afterlife and live accordingly! Because the following verse will apply there:

"On that Day, every person will flee from their own siblings, and their mother and father, and their spouse and children..." (Surah Abasa, Verses 34-36).

Everyone will account for their deeds. Think about that day. Prepare yourself accordingly. For that day, Allah says:

"Whether you reveal what is in your hearts or conceal it, Allah will call to you to account for it..." (Surah al-Baqarah, verse 284)

Know that the Almighty Allah is always close to you. Live knowing that there is no secret to Him.

Be one of those described as "On that day, there are some faces which are bright... Looking at their Lord..." (Surah Al-Qiyama, Verses 22-23).

Do sacrifice in this world to attain abundant blessings in the afterlife. The verse "They will be admitted to the heavens under which the rivers flow to stay there forever by the will of their Lord" (Surah Ibrahim, Verse 23) applies.

Do not get lost in the world. Allah Said, "This worldly life is no more than play and amusement..." (Surah Muhammed, Verse 36).

You have your own philosophy of living; you close your eyes to the truths and live as you find reasonable, but you forget one thing. For how long will you live like this? How will be your end? What happened to those before you? Did Allah create you for the world?

This world is temporary. You belong to the afterlife. You will stay there forever. This is how it is even if you don't find it reasonable.

There are many problems and sufferings in this world. Prefer the afterlife, work for it, so that you attain the eternal peace.

You should find grace when you are still in this world, because Allah says, "For THEM is good news in this world..." (Surah Yunus, Verse 64).

Make all the effort to obey the commands of Allah. Beg Allah to be successful. Do not follow your ego! Or it kills your heart and destroys you.

Take refuge to your Lord from your ego and its mentor, the satan. When your Lord helps you, the satan may not harm you.

The verse on this matters says: "...for indeed the soul is ever inclined to evil..."

(Surah Joseph, Verse 53).

Think about the afterlife, and do not fall for worldly blessings. Continue the remembrance (dhikr) of Allah as occasion serves. Open your inner eyes to see the truths, so that you can see the places that you visited in the past eternity before your eyes. Thus, you would understand that this world is nothing, and the divine lights will shine on your mirror of secret. You will start to see the realm of meanings without veils, and you will smell nice odors from the other realm.

Make effort to have your inner eyes open immediately, because Allah says, "Whoever is blind in this world will be blind in the afterlife..." (Surah Al-Isra, Verse 72).

So, repent Allah and try to fully perform your worships.

"He is the One who accepts repentance from His servants and forgives sins," (Surah Al Shura, Verse 25).

May Allah predestine all of us to spend our lives loyal to our repentance and to hopefully appear before our Lord with our deeds worthy for the afterlife.

OUR RELIGION AND OUR WORSHIPS

Our Almighty Creator created the universe and put it in order. The universe moves and proceeds within this order.

He created plants, animals, and men, and determined their reproduction and living conditions.

Among these creatures living on the Earth, He only gave intelligence and comprehension to man, and wanted to be known through him. He became the hearing ears, the seeing eyes and the speaking mouths of those who redeem and who are purified. He listened through their ears, looked through their eyes, and spoke through their mouths. Thus, it was again Him to watch the treasure He spread to the universe, and it was Him to explain. He made those who missed hear through those who had heard, see through those who had seen, and know through those who had known.

The All-Powerful Creator sent Prophets to the men who He created to make them live according to the purpose of creation and descended them scriptures through revelations.

Through His revelations and scriptures, He informed those who believed in Him about the rules to be followed. He called all these commands and prohibitions as religion. He named the obedience to the rules of the religion as worship. He wanted His servants to be cleansed and purified through plentiful charities and worships, and to become believers. Because, He said, "I would be the hearing ears, the seeing eyes, and the speaking mouths of my believing servants…" He wanted to hear, see, and talk through them.

Worships are required to know the reason of our creation and to reach the purpose of creation.

Worships are not unnecessary actions. Worshiping is cleansing and becoming purified. Only such people become believers and know the Creator. They live the truth of life.

Worship is the food of the spirit. It empowers our spiritual lives. Those who do not worship only nourish the body and become sensual; in other words, they live with selfishness and they don't think of others, but themselves. For them, life is about eating, drinking, and living comfortably. At the end, they leave without knowing why they were created and for what they lived.

Allah loves those who follows His orders and respects Him. He equips His beloved servant with His beautiful attributes. He makes them hear and see through Him, and to live in real terms.

Allah wants us to be nice and beautiful. This is only possible by following the commands of Allah. Because our Lord wishes the best for us.

Allah makes a sin recorded for our wrongdoings and a merit for our charities and good deeds. While He gives one sin for one wrongdoing, He givens ten merits to one good deed.

Our Prophet is Hazrat Muhammad Mustafa. He is the messenger and the true servant of Allah. He is the best practitioner of Allah's commands and the best to refrain from Allah's prohibitions. He is a role model who adopted the manners of Allah; and we need to adopt his manners and perform our worships like him so that we live the truth as a servant worthy of Allah.

Our religion is Islam. Our scripture is Qur'an. Islam has five pillars: The profession of faith (the Shahada), daily prayers (salat), fasting, giving alms (zakat), and pilgrimage (hajj).

Faith (iman) has six pillars: Belief in the existence and unicity of Allah; belief in the existence of angels; belief in the scriptures; belief in the Prophets; belief in the Judgment Day; and belief in the divine destiny.

If we want to live consistent with the purpose of creation and to have a beautiful afterlife, we need to believe in the pillars of faith, completely fulfill the pillars of Islam, and do plenty of favors and charities. We should meticulously follow the traditions (sunnah) of our Prophet.

We should not perform our worships casually, but in real terms, so that the change expected from is occurs. In this way, a person recovers from bad tempers, cleanses, and gets purified. He purifies his heart and gets to see the manifestation of Haqq. He becomes a role model by living the beauty and truth.

A person who wants to become a Muslim by fulfilling the pillars of Islam should first heartily believe in the meaning of "La ilaha illallah, Muhammadur rasulullah" without suspicion. Because our Prophet mentioned that shahada is one of the greatest sources of communication between Allah and the servant saying, "There is a veil between every creature and Allah. However, there are no veils between "La ilaha illallah," and a prayer of a father for his child." In another hadith, our Master says, "If anyone of you performs a nice ablution and says "Ashadu an la ilaha illallah wa ashadu an na Muhammadun abduhu ve rasuluhu," the eight doors of the heaven open to that person and he enters the heaven through the door he wishes…"

It is very important to incorporate the phrase of Tawhid (oneness of Allah) into our hearts, spirits, bodies, and our entire lives. Because the phrase of Tawhid had numerous benefits at the moment of death and in the grave just like its many benefits while living. For example, at the moment of death, Azrael appears in a nice semblance to the people of Tawhid, he brings odors from the heaven, and he takes their spirit without hurting them. In the grave, Munkar and Nakir appear in a nice semblance to such people, ask their questions without scaring them, an angel teaches them what they don't know, and Allah reminds them whatever they forget. Their graves fill with relief, light, and peace. Muslims, who enter the hell because their sins outweigh despite reciting the kalima shahada, are rather comfortable compared to others. They do not stay in the hell forever; once they complete their sentence for their sins and get cleansed, they are washed and cleansed in the Stream of Life, they get rid of the smell of the hell, and they enter into the heaven shining like a pearl.

Rumor has it that Hazrat Abraham asked Azrael how he appeared to non-believers when taking their lives and wanted to see Azrael in that form. Azrael asked, "O the Prophet of Allah! Can you tolerate this?" He answered, "Yes, I can tolerate this..." and Azrael told him to turn his head away. When Hazrat Abraham turned toward Azrael again, Azrael looked so scary and so dreadful that Hazrat Abraham was fainted out of fear. Upon he came to himself, he saw Azrael in his original image and said, "It is enough for evil people to see your face, even if nothing happens to them!"

There is no testing to the faithless. The true challenging test is for the perfect men. Those who keep their patience toward all sufferings, problems, and miseries of life, who preserve their faith, and who anchor in the Kalima Tawhid move up into a level where they can pass any test. After this, the believers should perform salat, fast, give zakat and pilgrimage, and they need to improve their morals, trust in, and surrender to Allah. Islam is to surrender. Our Almighty Creator loves nice people who get cleansed and purified. He wants to meet them. The true living is to know Him. It is to hear and see beyond the material.

We need to cleanse to worship. This is possible by cleaning our body from dirty objects and performing ablution of the whole body.

The first worship commanded by Allah to His servants is salat. The salat that we perform five times a day became an obligation on the Night of Ascension before the migration (hijra).

Qur'an puts great importance on salat. In Qur'an, salat is mentioned in almost hundred verses with words prayer, remembrance (dhikr), glorify, salat and the words formed this word stem. Many of these verses say, "Perform salat!" This emphasis on salat in Qur'an indicates its importance in the presence of Allah.

Qur'an has not clearly declared the number of units and the method to perform the obligatory salats. Muslims learned when and how to perform salat, the number of units, the procedure, and the manners of salat from our Prophet. Our Master told, "Perform your salat like I do!" and guided us on this matter. Our Prophet learned the practices related to salat from Gabriel.

Performing salat is the most important duty of a Muslim. However, salat does not only consist of a pattern. Qur'an mainly accentuates the meaning, importance, contents, and the purpose of salat rather than its pattern. In Qur'an, it is requested that the salat is performed with submission, the Muslims comprehend that they appear before Allah during salat, and that this awareness is maintained after salat.

Salat is the indication of a servant's sincerity In Qur'an, it is emphasized that the hypocrites perform salat without being lazy, and in order to show how indispensable salat is for Muslim individuals and society, how to perform salat even in a battlefield is described, and those who travel or who have excuses are asked to perform their salat by dry ablution with soil when they cannot find water.

Salat is the foundation of Islam. It is the essential worship. Performing the five-time daily prayers on time keeps a man away from all sins. Our Prophet and his companions continued to perform their salat altogether, even during battles. Despite the life-threatening risks, they didn't even think of abandoning salat and they preferred performing salat by risking their lives. Because they knew that only the One who had given them their lives had the power to protect them. They were trusting their lives to their true owner and performing the salat ordered by the One who created them.

Salat is the backbone of religion, and it has been greatly emphasized. It is commanded seventy times in Qur'an. There is no other worship mentioned and accentuated as much as salat. When our Prophet was asked, "Which is the favorite deed to Allah?" he said, "It is the salat performed when in due time!" and he declared that there was no worship superior to salat.

Our Prophet said, "This five-time salat is like a clear stream flowing in front of one's house. If that person bathes in this water five times a day, there is no dirt left on him, isn't it?"

Our Prophet indicated the importance of salat again by saying, "Salat is the backbone of the religion; the one who fails to perform salat demolishes his religion!"

All of the angels are at salat. Some of them are standing, some of them are bowing, some of them are prostrating, and some of them are sitting.

The faith of those who are against salat and who deliberately abandon it is in danger. Remember, the satan was dismissed from the presence of Allah for not following a single order of Allah.

Salat is the most significant mark that distinguishes us from non-Muslims; it is the identity of a Muslim. Regarding this matter, our Prophet said, "Salat is the trademark (the distinctive characteristic) between them and us!"

Every creature on the Earth has a duty. We benefit from the meat of some animals, the milk, the egg, and the power of some, etc. All these creatures have a purpose of creation. They are all created to serve and to make things easier for man. So, what man is created for? Every tree has a service and a fruit; then what is the fruit of man? The fruit of man is worship. Allah clearly declares why He created men and what He wants from them, "I did not create jinn and humans except to worship Me. I seek no provision from them, nor do I need them to feed Me. Indeed, Allah alone is the Supreme Provider, Lord of All Power, Ever Mighty!" (Surah Adh-Dhariyat, 56-58).

Salat is the ascension of a believer. In other words, the servant ascends to the presence of the Creator during salat and talks to Him at salat. In this sense, salat is the outcome of all worships. All worships are performed to appear in the presence of Haqq and to know Him.

Then, before starting to perform salat we need to intend to talk to Allah. We need to begin salat with this excitement and ask for ascension from Haqq.

We have to perform salat correctly and properly. We need to appear before Haqq in the way He asks.

Some scholars associate the reason for performing salat five times with the five senses of man. Because man sins with his five senses and performing salat five times is the redemption for the sins we committed with our five senses.

Every worship has a truth, a spirit just like everybody having a spirit. Without the spirit, the worships would be useless like the corpse.

The truth of salat is to recite the surah and to pray from the heart and with submission. Allah says in Qur'an, "Successful indeed are the believers: those who humble themselves in salat!" (Surah Al Mu'minun, Verses 1-2).

Sufis acknowledge the inner peace as the essential condition of salat. According to Sufis, it is mandatory to perform salat with submission to have the veils between Allah and the servant removed.

All the prophets, from Hazrat Adam to our Prophet, performed salat. Allah did not send a religion to the Earth without salat.

The servitude to Allah is not possible without following the religious rules. Therefore, our Prophet worshipped according to the religious rules of Prophet Abraham until he was honored with prophecy and salat and other worships became obligatory.

Qur'an gives examples from the prophets Jesus, Moses, Abraham, Noah, Zechariah, and notifies that salat and zakat were ordered to them as well. To give an example to some of them: "So the angels called out to him while he stood praying in the sanctuary..." (Surah Ali Imran, Verse 39).

The words of Prophet Jesus spoken as a little baby are written in Quran as follows: "Jesus declared, "I am truly a servant of Allah. He has destined me to be given the Scripture and to be a prophet. He has made me a blessing wherever I go and bid me to establish salat and give zakat tax as long as I live, and to be kind to my mother!" (Surah Maryam, Verses 30, 31). This is one of the most obvious evidence indicating that salat is not a worship specific to Islam brought by Hazrat Muhammed (pbuh), and it was in all religions including Christianity.

We do not know when and how the salat was performed, how many units were there, or which prayers were recited during salat in religions before Islam. There are no certain explanations about these neither in Qur'an not in the hadiths. Qur'an does not discuss the details or give the dates of the incidents. Yet, we clearly understand from Qur'an that salat has been ordered to all men ever existed, and all the Prophets as well as those who believed in them performed salat.

Salat is the worship which is denied first by the unbelievers and for which they will regret first for denying on the Day of Judgment. "…Of the sinners, "What has landed you in Hell?" They will reply, "We were not of those who performed salat." (Surah Al Muddaththir, Verses 41-43).

Salat was ordered by the first verses of Surah Muzzammil. A year later, the final verses of the same surah indicated that night salat was obligatory exclusively to our Prophet: "Surely your Lord knows that you O Prophet stand in salat for nearly two-thirds of the night, or sometimes half of it, or a third, as do some of those with you. Allah alone keeps a precise measure of the day and night. He knows that you believers are unable to endure this and has turned to you in mercy. So, recite in salat whatever you can from the Qur'an… And continue to perform regular salats, pay zakat, and lend to Allah a good loan…" (Surah Muzzammil, Verse 20).

It is narrated that on the early days of Islam, Gabriel taught our Prophet how to perform ablution and salat, and he taught these to his wife, Khadija, and the other companions who converted to Islam. Our Prophet and other Muslims performed their salat secretly outside

Mecca for some time to avoid the torture of Qureshis. Later, our Prophet started to perform salat openly, and thereupon, Abu Jahl threatened the Messenger of Allah and tried to prevent him from performing salat. This is explained in Qur'an as follows: "Have you seen the man who prevents a servant of Ours (the Prophet) from praying? What if this servant is rightly guided, or encourages righteousness? What if that man persists in denial and turns away? Does he not know that Allah sees all?" (Surah Al Alaq, Verses 9-14).

Unlike other verses, Allah did not send Gabriel to the Earth for the verses related to making salat obligatory. On the Night of Ascension, He ascended our Prophet and accepted him in His presence and made that glorious offer Himself. We can also understand from this incident that salat is far more different and special than other worships.

That night, fifty-time salat was made obligatory. Then, upon the request of our Prophet, it was decreased to five times and Allah said to our Prophet: "O Muhammed! The truth is that the promises and decrees before me do not change. This five-time salat has merit equal to fifty times."

On the Night of Ascension, Gabriel incised the chest of the Messenger of Allah and washed it with zamzam apparently and inwardly. When our Prophet ascended, he reached the level "qurb" (proximity to Allah) and he was offered numerous treats and blessings. He was so delighted with this proximity that he said, "O Allah! Do not send me to the world, which is home to evilness for the second time, do not make me fall into the mesh of nature and whim!" Allah said:

"Our decree is that you shall return to the world to complete the religion as We will give you the same things (in salat) as We have given you here!" After returning to the world, whenever the Prophet of Allah missed Allah and that glorious station, he used to say, "O Bilal, move on and call us for salat, and ease us with salat!"

Each salat had been a reunion and an ascension for him. People saw his body when he was performing salat; but, his spirit was in salat, his inner heart was supplicating, his secret was ascending, and his ego was melting. He was bodily a human, but his spirit was at the station of talking to Allah.

One does not forget Allah in salat, but he does what is required to appear in His presence. On this matter, our Prophet said, "There are many people whose share from salat is nothing but distress and suffering!"

Do not allow your hearts to be heedless while your bodies are at salat. Forget about anything at salah, but Allah. In this respect, our Prophet expressed, "Allah does not heed a salat where the heart is not present!"

If we consider salat as a facility provided by Allah to His servants who want to go to Him rather than a distress or suffering, and if we remember that we will be attending the call of and meeting the Sultan of the hearts inviting us to His presence five times a day, we will understand that this is not a distressing duty, but a reward.

Hazrat Aisha said, "The Messenger of Allah spoke to us. We spoke to him, as well. When the time for salat came, he said he did not recognize us. This is because of his engagement with the magnificence and greatness of Allah and his attachment to Allah!" When Hazrat Ali was about to begin performing salat, his body begun shaking and his face discolored. He used to say, "It is time to take over the trust which was offered to the seven-fold skies and the earth, and which they failed to bear!"

While performing ablution, repent your sins and clean your heart, then perform salat by picking a proper clothing.

Listen to the call for salat carefully and feel it in your heart. When the call for salat starts, stop talking and stop doing whatever you are doing. After the call for salat, perform your salat with the community if possible.

Before beginning the salat, you need to turn your face toward Qibla and your heart toward Allah. Our Prophet said, "The one who stands for salat and whose intention, face and heart are with Allah is like a newborn; that is to say, he is cleansed of all sins'."

In this regard, the value of the salat decreases if one turns his heart away from Allah and he is occupied with something else. To avoid your heart being occupied with other things, it would be useful for many people to perform salat in a silent and dim setting. To avoid distraction, remove eye-catching objects from the place where you will prostrate or perform your salat elsewhere.

If you have an uncompleted task, first finish it, and then perform your salat. To this respect, our Prophet said, "When the meal is ready and it is time for salat, first have your meal…" Apart from this, to prevent your heart from being occupied with other things, keep it busy with the meanings of the surah and glorifications recited. If the heart is occupied with health problems, take the necessary medication, and be treated.

To perform the salat nicely, our Prophet recommended to think of death during salat. As he also mentioned, death eliminates the worldly pleasures. If you cannot stop being occupied with worldly affairs and whims, thinking of death would help you to avoid such ideas. There should be existence in standing, honoring in bowing, and nothingness in prostration. The heart of salat is prostration. The servant must reach nothingness in prostration. Our Almighty Creator fills in every nothingness with His existence. The servant reaches Haqq with his nothingness. In other words, whoever vanishes, finds Haqq.

When our Creator asked our Prophet about what he brought Him during the Ascension, our Prophet answered, "I brought You my nothingness!" which is an indication of this matter.

Come on, you too jump into the ocean like a droplet, vanish within and become the ocean to ascend during salat and to appear in the presence and take over the trust like Hazrat Ali did!

While reciting Tashahud in the presence of Haqq that you found when you lost yourself and disappeared in prostration, talk to Haqq from the same mouth. Because Tashahud is the talk between our Prophet and Haqq during the ascension.

I have found the soul of souls, let my soul is taken
I have forgotten gain and loss, let my shop looted

I have passed beyond my very self and removed the veils from my eyes
I reached the Friend, let my doubts disappear

My ego left me; the Friend covered my entire possession
I reached placelessness, let my place be plundered

I have broken off everything and flown toward the Friend
I have fallen into the council of love, let my council be ravaged

I am tired of duality and satisfied with the treat of oneness
I drank the wine of suffering, let my remedy be spoiled

The Friend has come to us to be seen in the world of existence
The ruined heart has been filled with light, let my universe be destroyed

I have given up my endless desires and wishes
I have tired of summer and winter
I have found the real garden, let my garden be dug out

Yunus, you say it nice and sweet
I have found the honey of the honeys, let my hive looted

– Yunus Emre

Giving zakat is one of the pillars of Islam. Our Prophet said, "Islam is built on five pillars: La ilaha illallah Muhammadur resulullah; salat; zakat; fasting; pilgrimage…"

Zakat is calculated over the gold, silver, livestock, and commodities. While giving zakat, one must absolutely intend to do so.

Zakat also has a truth just like the truth and the soul of salat. Without knowing its truth and essence, zakat would be like an image without spirit or truth.

Loving Allah more than anything, even more than your life, is one of the most beautiful qualities of believers. Only telling that you love is insufficient. The one, who does not abandon his loved ones for His sake, may not thoroughly love Him. Wealth and properties are things men love. By commanding to give zakat, Allah is testing us with our loved ones. In this regard, Qur'an says: "O Muhammed! Say, "If your fathers and children and siblings and spouses and extended family and the wealth you have acquired and the trade you fear will decline and the homes you cherish are more beloved to you than Allah and His Messenger and struggling in His Way, then wait until Allah brings about His Will. Allah does not guide the rebellious people." (Surah Tawba, Verse 24)

Everyone claims to love Allah very much. However, when one is told to give from his property for His sake, he finds this difficult and does not want to give. This shows the degree of one's faith.

There are three groups of those giving zakat: The first one is the truthful ones (siddiq). They sacrifice all that they have for the sake of Allah. Hazrat Abu Bakr was one of the truthful ones (siddiq). He was very wealthy. He spends all his riches on the way of Allah. When the Messenger of Allah asked him, "What did you leave to your family?" he answered, "I left them Allah and His messenger!"

The second one is the group of righteous ones (salihun). The righteous ones are the servants loved by Allah. They do not give away their properties at once; however, they never rely on their properties. When the time comes, they help those who are in need and give from their properties. They consider themselves equal to the poor, and they do not boast. The third group is the nice people. They give away one fortieth of their wealth. In other words, they do what is obligatory (fard). They fulfill the command willingly, relishingly and timely. They are also acceptable servants. Because, for those who do not hand out fortieth of their tangible assets provided by Allah to the needy upon His command, it is not possible to claim that they love Allah.

Zakat cleanses the hearts by removing the dirt of stinginess within the hearts. Stinginess is a bad disease which prevents you from being close to Allah.

Giving zakat is praising the blessings bestowed. Salat, fasting and pilgrimage are being grateful for the body given as a blessing. Zakat is being grateful for the property given as blessing.

The worship of the one who knows these truths is saved from being a meaningless semblance.

You need to rush to give zakat. We should not postpone it by following the delusions of the satan. It is the best to give it before a year runs out. Because giving once a year runs out is mandatory.

So, giving with a delay is not out of love, but fear. Besides, the zakat given early makes the hearts of the poor delighted earlier.

Unless you rush giving your zakat, the satan may dissuade us through various tricks.

Giving more zakat during the months Ramadan and Muharram is a nice behavior. Because these months are sacred. The more precious the time of giving zakat is, the more merit it has.

One of the most important aspects about zakat is confidentiality. Zakat may be given openly to be a good example to others; however, it is hard and important for the giver to keep away from pride, arrogance, and selfness.

You should not expect the one to whom you give zakat to be grateful to and respect you. In reality, the poor makes you a favor by accepting your zakat and saves you from being punished. They are the ones to be grateful for. You need to thank them.

Zakat is given to the poor. Finding the true poor and giving zakat to them increases the merit of the zakat. The poor that you are looking for may be a person who is studying, who hides his poverty and only asks from Allah, who is sick or who has a crowded family, or that person may be one of our relatives.

Apart from zakat, you may give alms to the poor from your money, properties, food, and beverage. Alms is the remedy for every problem. Whatever your intention for giving is, Allah would not reject your wish. As long as you give it sincerely without showing off or humiliating or hurting anyone.

Our Prophet said: "Give alms, even if it is a date. Because it revives the poor and removes the sins like the water putting out the fire." He also said: "Tomorrow, on the Judgment Day, until there is a judgment among people, everyone stays in the shadow of their alms." When he was asked, "Which alms are more virtuous?" he said, "The alms given when one is health, has hope of living, and when one does not afraid of poverty. They are not those which you call "This is for the one, that is for the other one" after you wait for death to come.

The one has already taken it even if you say or nor!" In another hadith, our Master said, "Anyone who provides some clothing to a Muslim is under the protection of Allah as long as that man continues to wear that cloth…" and expressed the significance of giving alms.

The alms given sincerely and secretly without hypocrisy and show-off put out the rage and anger of Allah.

Our Prophet said, "The alms first drop into the hand of grace of Allah and then into the hand of the poor…" So, in truth we are giving the alms to Allah and the poor becomes the deputy of Allah while taking it. Then, the alms should be given in embarrassment and kindness, not by taunting or despising!

Fasting is also one of the pillars of Islam. Regarding fasting, our Prophet said:

"Allah says: Each favor is rewarded with ten times. But fasting is reserved for Me, I reward it Myself."

"Patience is the half of faith. And, fasting is the half of patience."

"The breath odor of a person fasting is nicer than the smell of musk in the sight of Allah."

"Even the sleep of someone fasting is a worship."

Allah says, "My servant gave up eating and drinking only for Me; only I can reward it!" Even though all worships are for Him, this like Him calling Kaaba, "My home!" when the entire universe is His property.

The truth of fasting is abandoning wishes and desires by keeping away from eating and drinking. Because hunger cuts lust and desires off. In this regard, our Prophet said, "Satan circulates within human body like blood. Block his passageway with hunger!"

Besides, he warned about this saying, "Unless a person abandons speaking bad words and occupying him with useless things, there is nothing left to him from his fasting except for hunger and thirst!"

Fasting is performed during Ramadan. This worship is fulfilled by keeping away from eating, drinking and sexual intercourse. This is the fasting of common people. The fasting of special people is to prevent the heart from being occupied with anything but Allah and to avoid engaging it in worldly things during fasting. Additionally, they abstain themselves from looking at anything that would darken the heart, speaking unnecessary words, listening to harmful subjects, and keeping all organs from committing a sin.

Our Prophet used to perform union fasting when he wanted to come together with Allah. Fasting allows reaching Allah, the giver of blessings through His blessings. In this sense, Allah addressed the friend of Haqq saying, "I created food so that you can eat Me; I created beverages so that you can drink Me!" (Perfect Man - Abd al-Karim al-Jili)

Pilgrimage is also one of the pillars of Islam. A person who has the means should go on pilgrimage for once in his life.

Regarding pilgrimage, our Prophet said: "There are many sins that may only be forgiven by stopping by and standing on Mount Arafat."

"A person who leaves home with the intention to pilgrimage and dies on his way is given the merit of one pilgrimage and one omre for each year until the Judgment Day. The one who dies in Mecca will neither be interrogated nor called to account."

"An acceptable pilgrimage is better than the world and anything in the world. Its reward may only be the heaven."

"There is no greater sin for one than assuming that his sins are not forgiven after stopping by and standing on Mount Arafat."

"The satan looks more vile, inferior and wan on the eve than any other day. Because, on the eve, Allah scatters His mercy on His servants and forgives many great sins."

Pilgrimage is like the journey to the afterlife. The candidate pilgrim bids farewell to his family and friends and visits his Protector by going to Allah's house. This resembles the separation at the time of death.

While a merit acquired anywhere around the world is rewarded with tenfold, a merit acquired in Kaaba is rewarded with hundred thousand merits. Of course, this applies to sins as well. Therefore, we should be very careful of every step we make there. In this regard, our Prophet said: "If a person does not speak bad words or get stuck in sin during pilgrimage, he would be free from sins as on day of his birth." Therefore, it was forbidden to scuffle, hurt people, torture people, or speak bad words on pilgrimage. If you do not pay attention to these matters, you will return home with so much more sins and far from being relieved from your sins. Eventually, the pilgrimage would not touch your spirit and it does not give you anything except for fatigue and distress.

After being removed from heaven, Hazrat Adam was descended to a region called Serendib (Ceylon Island) and Hazrat Eve to Jeddah. They started to search for each other and finally, they met in Arafat.

Later, Allah asked Adam to build a house for Him on the earth and sent an angel to show the location of that house and to teach the worships to be performed during pilgrimage.

After building the House of Allah, Adam prayed: "O Lord, forgive anyone from my generation who admits his sins like I do."

Allah responded to him, "O Adam, as the compensation of the House of Allah, I will forgive those who circumambulate it!"

The most precious worship on the earth is salat. However, the most precious worship in Kaaba is circumambulation, because our Prophet said, "One hundred twenty graces descend on the House of Allah; sixty of them is for those circumambulating, forty for those performing salat, and twenty for those watching the House of Allah!"

There are many wisdoms (hikmah) regarding the location of Kaaba, which is not easily accessible, green, or spacious. If so, people would go there for vacation or for a touristic trip. But now, people go to that region which lacks any natural beauties, and which consists only of stones, soil, and arid lands just to visit the house of Allah and to fulfill His commands. They endure any hardship to receive His consent.

Allah ordered Abraham to live around the House of Allah with his wife Hagar and his little son Ismail. He followed the ordered of Allah and set off with his wife and son. Gabriel was guiding them.

In every wetland and greenery, they passed by on their way, Hazrat Abraham asked whether they would settle there. They finally reached the location where the Zamzam Well is situated today. Gabriel told them that they would stay there.

While Hazrat Abraham was returning after leaving his wife and little baby there, Hagar shouted behind his back: "Where are you going by leaving us here all alone?" Abraham didn't say a word and he continued walking. Hagar ran after and reached him, and asked, "Did Allah order this?" When Abraham affirmed, Hagar took heart and said, "Then, Allah will not allow us to get lost, He will protect us..."

Hagar took her son in her arms and sat under a tree. Sometime later, they ran out of food and water. Hazrat Ismail got hungry and began to cry. Thereupon, Hagar get into a flap and ran toward Safa Hill leaving her baby under a tree. She looked around, but she sees neither a person nor a living thing. In panic, she ran toward Marwa Hill. When she came to the level area between two hills, she couldn't see her child. Therefore, she accelerated there, and she ran toward the opposite hill until she could see her son. She could neither see anyone there. She ran from one hill to the other like that for seven times. Just as she was about to lose hope, she saw a man near her baby and she immediately went toward him. It was Gabriel that she saw. He told Hagar not to be afraid and he stomped on the ground. Water spurt from where he stomped. Seeing the water, Hagar became very happy, but she shouted, "Zam, zam! (Stop, stop!)" as she feared that her child would drown. So, the zamzam water cropped out.

Hazrat Hagar and Hazrat Ismail began living around that water. When the neighboring Curhum tribe learned about the water spurted, they asked permission to settle there. Thus, the city of Mecca was established.

When Abraham wanted to see his wife Hagar and his son Ismail, he got on Buraq, traveled long miles to go to Mecca for one day, and returned his home in Damascus at night.

When Hazrat Ismail turned seven, Hazrat Abraham had a dream. In his dream, he was sacrificing his son, Hazrat Ismail.

Thereupon, he immediately got on Buraq and went to Mecca. He told his son, "Take a big knife and a rope, son. Then, come with me to the valley over there..." and he and his son set off.

On their way, the satan told Hazrat Abraham, "Are you crazy? Will you murder your son because of a dream? It should be the satan disguised to make you murder your son!" Hazrat Abraham understood that it was the satan; he picked a stone and threw to him. He said, "Go away, the cursed satan. You may not prevent me from fulfilling Allah's command!"

Failed to get a result from Hazrat Abraham, the satan went to Hagar and asked, "Abraham will murder your son. What are you doing here?" Hazrat Hagar said, "Would a father hurt his child? Why would he murder his son?" The satan replied, "He saw a dream and he think Allah asked him to sacrifice his son. How could a man murder his son because of a dream?"

Hagar also understood that it was the satan. She also picked a stone and threw it saying, "Go away, the cursed satan! You may not deceive me. If this is Allah's order, then Abraham fulfills it, and no one can prevent him from this!"

The satan understood that he could not deceive her either and went to Hazrat Ismail. "O Ismail! Your father is going to kill you and he thinks that Allah ordered this. Will you allow him to do so?" Hazrat Ismail replied, "My father won't hurt me; however, if this is the order of Allah, there is no escape, and I will be honored to be sacrificed for Him!" and he picked a stone and threw it to the satan.

So, the satan was stoned in Mina for the first time.

Hazrat Abraham lied his son on the ground and moved the razor-edged knife on his son's throat. But the knife did not cut. At that point,

Gabriel descended on the earth with a ram, and Allah called out to them:

"O Abraham! You showed loyalty to your dream! Here is a ram for you to sacrifice instead of your son! Slaughter it!"

Thereupon, Abraham told his son, "Stand up, son! A ransom was descended for you!" and he sacrificed that ram in Mina.

There is circumambulation in all prophets. However, Kaaba has been demolished for several times until today, and even its foundation was lost during Noah's flood.

From then on, Allah ordered Hazrat Abraham to rebuild Kaaba. So, he went to Mecca. Hagar had died when he reached there. He told his son Ismail, "My Lord orders me to rebuild the House of Allah here!" and they started building Kaaba together.

Gabriel helped them with the construction of Kaaba and taught them their duty of pilgrimage. Then, Hazrat Abraham heard an exclamation for Allah, saying: "O the Khalil Prophet, call people for pilgrimage." Hazrat Abraham asked, "O Lord, how can I make myself heard by people?" Allah answered him, "O Khalil, your duty is to call, and making you heard is on Me! You call out, and I will publicize your invitation…"

Hazrat Abraham stood on a stone called the Maqam Ibrahim (the Station of Abraham). The stone rose up higher and higher, the mountains, stones, plains, seas became smaller and smaller, and shutting his ears with his fingers, he said:

"O people! Your Lord has a house, and He is commanding you to pilgrimage. O people! Circumambulating Kaaba is obligatory to you. O people! Obey Allah. O the servants of Allah, follow the invitation of your Lord!"

He addressed with such love and affection that the stone under his feet melted and his footprints remained on the stone.

The following words were heard from all the creatures and from all the beings hearing Hazrat Abraham's invitation:

"Labbayk! Allahumma labbayk! *Here I am [at your service]! O Allah! Here I am [at your service]!)*

Labbayka la shareeka laka Labbayk! *(Here I am [at your service], You have no partners, here I am [at your service]!)*

Inna'l-hamd wal ni'mata laka wa'l mulk. *(All praises and all blessings belong to You. All sovereignty belongs to You.)*

La shareeka lak. *(You have no partner).*

It is said that ninety-nine prophets are lying in the courtyard of Kaaba between Maqam Ibrahim and the Zamzam Well. Hagar and Hazrat Ismail are lying beneath the Hijr. So, the graves of hundred prophets in total are located there.

Actually, Hijr is included in the area of Kaaba. When Kaaba was first built, it covered the Hijr. But when it was rebuilt during the time of our Prophet, it was built smaller due to financial impossibilities and lack of material, and the "Hijr" was left outside. If a person swears, "I performed salat inside the Kaaba!" after performing salat at the Hijr, that person is telling the truth. Today, Hijr is the area outside the Kaaba which is surrounded by a wall.

The pilgrims begin to circumambulate at the corner where Hajar al Aswad is located. Hajar al Aswad means the Black Stone. This stone was descended from the heaven.

Abraham told his son Ismail to bring a nice stone and to place it as a sign of the starting point of circumambulation of the pilgrims. However, Ismail did not find the stones he brought worthy to Kaaba. Just then, Gabriel brought a stone from the heaven and place it on the wall. When this stone first arrived, it was pearl white. The Messenger of

Allah said, "When Allah descended this stone from the heaven, it was whiter than milk. But the sins of people blackened it!"

Regarding the Black Stone, our Master said, "The Black Stone is like the right hand of Allah reaching to His servants…"

It is a merit to look at the Kaaba. It gives peace to the heart and cleanses the eyes and the heart. Besides, if we manage to look at it with our inner eyes without blinking, then the veils will be removed, the unseen will be seen, and the secrets will be attained. The one looking at it loses himself and attains his own secret.

You should not talk while looking at the Kaaba. Looking at Kaaba is a worship. One should not talk while looking at Kaaba, just like he is not talking in salat.

Kaaba is the place of Allah's gaze. It is a place where Allah constantly gazes on the earth. If you look at Kaaba with your inner eyes, the veils in between remove, and our sight meets the host.

We want to come to you,
O Lord, may You not forsake us!
You know we love you,
O Lord, may You not forsake us!

You are the sultan of the hearts
You are the remedy for the sufferers
You are the wish of the lovers
O Lord, may You not forsake us!

You made Khalil Ibrahim built a house
You made him invite Your servants to that house
You made Your visitors reach Your grace
O Lord, may You not forsake us!

How may we come without You wish us to
We may not go that long distance unless You want us to
We cry with Your longing
O Lord, may You not forsake us!
Your lover wants you
Grace us and show Your beauty
These humble servants wish to come to You
O Lord, may You not forsake us!

We always repeat Your name
Our eyes filled with tears
We paled with Your longing
O Lord, may You not forsake us!

You show mercy to Your servants
O Lord, may You not forsake us!
You do not refuse those who want You
O Lord, may You not forsake us!

– Faruk Dilaver

PRAYER

Allah addresses His servants through revelation or inspiration. He addresses the Messengers through revelation and His beloved servants through inspiration. In return, people may also address God. This is only possible through praying. For someone to address Allah, he should reach an extraordinary state.

However, this state may be attained by being completely isolated from others and the world. Such a person may no more perceive anything. When the isolation is completed, man can address Allah.

A man in this state is different than ordinary people. He turns into a creature superior to his own being.

When a man addresses Allah and asks for help in this extraordinary state, this is the true prayer.

The reasons which put one into this situation may differ. These are: the profound love and yearning to God, an incident, disease, severe hunger, and thirst threatening one with death.

People pray their Lord in such times of danger by reaching this extraordinary state. But once the danger disappears, they forget about it. Allah does not like this. Remembering your state in such difficult times, recalling it under normal conditions, and praying Allah by entering that state would be correct. Thus, you would join the ones whose prays are accepted.

When a man's heart moves away from worldly wishes and desires, this extraordinary state occurs.

For example, a person with a fatal disease is not affected by the worldly wishes and desires. A patient in this state would easily switch to the state mentioned above, and he may make a true prayer by addressing Allah.

Prayer is heart's talk with Allah. When the heart is cleansed and becomes exalted, it addresses Allah.

Once the difficult conditions suffered by a person disappear, if that person continues addressing Allah without impairing his state, then his prayer turns into worship. Prayer is the essence of worship.

Prayer is not repeating the words memorized, but a sincere supplication. Our Prophet prayed every day throughout his life. Prayer has a great importance for him.

Prayer prevents the current and possible disasters and calamities. Under such conditions, what falls to us is to pray constantly. Accidents may only be avoided by prayer.

We need to pray a lot in times of welfare and abundance so that Allah accepts our prayers in difficult times.

Allah is pleased when one asks for all his needs from Him. Allah decides whether to fulfill one's need or not. There is no objection to this. Any objection would lead to rebellion.

Allah accepts all prayers that are for the good of a person. However, He responds some of them in this life and the others in the afterlife.

When the servant says, "Oh my Lord!" Allah answers, "Tell me, my servant, what do you want?" Hearing this reply by the heart is a great grace.

Allah is not pleased with those who do not pray Him and tell about their status.

Prayers vary in kind based on different places and times. We may review and learn about them from the hadiths of our Prophet.

Prayer is not only for the weak, the odd or the helpless, but also those who are in condition should pray a lot.

When a man incurs a damage, he should pray while he is sitting, lying on one side, and standing.

Actually, the universe is praying with the entire creation. They are glorifying Him. However, we may not understand their worships. They all have different prostrations and worships.

The societies which abandon praying never get better. In the past, many societies disappeared altogether because of this.

We should pray a lot for our family, friends, country, and the world. Because there is a great need for this.

Each calamity that happens is related to previous actions. Therefore, we need to ask for forgiveness from Allah without delay and pray Him to forgive us.

You must start praying by turning toward Qibla and turning your palms toward your face without looking at the sky.

At the moment of prayer, we need to be sincere, serious, and decent. One prays better in isolated and silent places.

The prayers made for others are accepted more quickly. Because they are free of selfishness.

Prayers should be made with a low voice, from the inside and with hope that they will be accepted.

What makes prayer possible is believing that it would be accepted. When this belief weakens, the extraordinary state of the praying person spoils.

Man is saved from the most desperate problems or the most fatal diseases through prayer as long as he absolutely believes that he will be saved. Because God has the power to do anything.

One should continue praying on the same matter again and again. Our Prophet used to pray at least three times when he had a wish.

May Allah put us into the group of people whose prayers are not rejected. May He make our ending nice and easy.

SUFISM

Every religion has an order which deepens and develops the aspects of heart, spirit, and morals. In our religion, this is called Sufism. Sufism is the science of inner heart; it allows growing mature men by cleansing and beautifying the inner heart. This is the science of comprehension and behavior.

Sufism is to abandon all bad tempers and actions, and to take nice and beautiful ones.

Sufism is taking out everything other than Allah from the heart and building hopes only on Allah.

Sufism is a method of warning to be conscious about religious matters.

In our belief, the mature and the perfect man is our Prophet Muhammed Mustafa (pbuh). He is Insan Kamil (the Perfect Man). We may also mature by imitating him in terms of the heart, spirit, and the morals. To the extent that we resemble him, we can hear what he heard; we can see what he saw; and we can experience what he experienced.

For this, we should first love him more than our parents, more than everything we have - even from our lives, and we should mature by fulfilling the requirements of Sufism which is the science of imitating him.

Sufism is the knowledge of transferring. It has been transferred from eye to the heart and from the heart to the eye since our Prophet. It was our Prophet who first practiced and lived this knowledge. He is the role model. Those who witnessed his life and practices transferred these through their states and behaviors to those who didn't see him. Then those who saw the ones who had seen him continued to transfer. Thus, these states and behaviors reached today.

The first wise teacher (murshid), role model is our Prophet. One who sees him is like he has seen Allah. Because he is the mirror of Haqq. The beauty of Haqq manifests from his face.

There are four stages for believers. Islamic law (sharia), order of Sufism (tariqa), truth (haqiqa), gnosis (marifa). Sharia refers to all the commands of Allah and the traditions (sunnah) of our Prophet. Tariqa is the way of practicing Sufism. Sharia is the body of the religion, and Sufism is the spirit. The body without the spirit is corpse. Tariqa is also the garden of the truth. Sharia is the gate to that garden. Those who do not follow sharia may not proceed to tariqa. Those who do not follow tariqa may not proceed to haqiqa. Those who may not find haqiqa may not obtain knowledge.

The friends of Allah explained that what is permissible in sharia is a small sin in tariqa; what is a small sin in tariqa is a great sin in haqiqa; and what is a great sin in haqiqa is blasphemy.

One can proceed from sharia to haqiqa through Sufism. Sufism and sharia are not separate things. Sufism is the path of reunion. The statement in Surah al-Fatihah, "You alone we worship!", is sharia, and "You alone we ask for help!" is Sufism.

Sharia covers all commands and prohibitions of Allah. They are the religious values regulating man's life. In this regard, they are the religious rules including all the verses, hadiths and sunnah. In His

Book Allah says, "...To each of you We have ordained a code of law and a way of life..." (Surah al-Ma'idah, verse 48).

People put their lives in order by following the divine will through sharia. Sharia is related to all behaviors of people. Allah states this in His Book with the verse "Now We have set you on the clear Way of faith. So, follow it, and do not follow the desires of those who do not know!" (Surah al-Jathiyah, verse 18).

Tariqa is the method of practicing Sufism; it is a path and a procedure. Tariqa is a discipline. It is reaching the essence of the religion and finding Haqq and truth by adhering to the principles of sharia. This is a path of spiritual struggle and abstinence.

Facing towards Allah, concentration and consent through repentance, asceticism, trust, contentment, seclusion, remembrance, and surrender constitute the basis of Sufism.

As a Sufism term, tariqa is the path followed to reach Haqq. According to a Sufi, the number of paths leading to Allah is equal to the number of breaths inhaled and exhaled by all people.

Haqiqa means belonging to Haqq. Anything other than Haqq is called "maasiwa." Haqiqa is to turn your heart from maasiwa to Haqq. Sharia, tariqa, and haqiqa are a whole. Sharia is worshipping Allah; tariqa is wanting Allah; and haqiqa is observing Allah.

Marifa is heart's knowledge of life. A heart without marifa is dead. Marifa is to know Allah. The sources of marifa are the heart, spirit, inspiration, and revelation. The sources of knowledge are intellect, feelings, and transfer. In this sense, knowledge and marifa are different from each other. Those with knowledge are called scholar, and those with marifa are called wise.

As Yunus Emre says, "Sharia is the path of tariqa for those who reach. Haqiqa and marifa are beyond it..."

Our Prophet said, "Sharia is my words; tariqa is my state; and haqiqa is my capital!"

In other words, he intended to mean that "I follow sharia pursuant to my testament to Allah, but my current state is to be stable on the path to Allah. My destination is HAQIQA which was predestined to me in the past-eternity."

Necmettin Kubra said, "Sharia is like a vessel, tariqa is like the sea. Marifa is the knowledge to reach the pearl in the sea, and haqiqa is the pearl itself. The pearl is the contentment, heaven, and the Beauty of Allah. The one who wants the pearl should get on that vessel and sail so that he can reach that pearl..."

The realms are the manifestation of the divine names and attributes. Pursuant to the verse "...Day in and day out He has something to bring about!" (Surah ar-Rahman, verse 29)

the names and attributes of Allah have no limits. He has infinite manifestations. He manifests in a different way to all His servants.

Haqq is the existence in all eternity. Those existing other than Haqq come to existence with His absolute existence. All creatures become apparent from the absolute existence of Haqq.

According to a hadith, when people enter the heaven, Haqq will show them His beauty, and when He makes Himself apparent saying, "I am your Lord who you have been longing to see for so many years!" but the people of heaven will deny and cry out. Haqq will appear in three different semblances, and they will deny again. Finally, Allah will ask them, "Is there any sign or signal between you and your Lord?" They will say, "Yes, there is!" Thereupon, Allah will manifest and appear as per their beliefs and presumptions. Then, they will see and accept. However, the wise ones will acknowledge and accept as soon as they see. Because they get to know Haqq in this world by gathering all beliefs. Therefore, Allah says in Qur'an, "But whoever is blind to Haqq in this world will be blind in the Hereafter, and even far more astray from seeing Haqq!" (Surah al-Isra, Verse 72).

A wise man knows his own truth by being dependent to a person who attained his own truth and by adopting his morals. In this sense, Surah al-Ma'idah, Verse 35 says, "If you want to find Me, there are My servant who has found me. Hold on to them. They lead you and make you reach Me!" This is the interpretation of Ismael Hakkı Bursevi. Actually, one should know no matter what he glorifies or worships, in reality he worships Haqq. Because Haqq made Himself the reality of every creature to prevent people from glorifying and worshiping anything other than Him.

The interpretation of the verse, "For your Lord has decreed that you worship none but Him…" (Surah al-Isra, verse 23) is as follows: "O Muhammed! Your Lord has decreed and appreciated that you do not worship anyone except Him. Neither the worship nor affection or glorification belongs to anyone else. Such that, the one worshiping an idol worships the Eternal Refuge, namely Allah in reality. Because the existence of the idol comes from the Eternal Refuge, namely from Allah. Then, be it known that existence belongs to Haqq. This is certain."

The interpretation of the verse, "To Allah belong the east and the west, so wherever you turn you are facing towards Allah…" (Surah al-Baqarah, Verse 115) is as follows: "Wherever one turns, the face of Haqq is there both in apparent and hidden manners. Haqq shows a beauty on every face, a coyness in every beauty, an apparition in every coyness, and love in every apparition. He does not limit Himself with a single face."

Haqq becomes apparent when certainty comes. And certainty belongs to Allah. There are three types of certainty:

- Knowledge of Certainty
- Eye of Certainty
- Truth of Certainty

Knowledge of certainty is to know; eye of certainty is to see; and truth of certainty is to become. With regards to becoming, Allah says in a holy saying, "I was sick; yet you didn't come to ask after me. I got hungry; yet you didn't feed me!"

Those who have a sound grasp of the truth are called the wise, saints of Allah, and men of Allah. These are the people referred to in the verse, "There will certainly be no fear for the friends of Allah, nor will they grieve!" (Surah Jonah, Verse 62).

When Allah, the One and the Dominant, appears to a servant with His attribute of dominance, all the creatures and himself disappears from the sight of that servant pursuant to the verses, "...Everything is bound to perish except He Himself...!" (Surah al-Qasas, Verse 88), and "Every being on earth is bound to perish. Only your Lord Himself, full of Majesty and Honor, will remain forever!" (Surah ar-Rahman, Verses 26-27). Thus, that person reaches the stage of Annihilation in Allah. Allah, the Almighty, asks him, "Who does all authority belong to this Day?" As he does not exist, The Creator answers with all His magnificence, "To Allah—the One, the Supreme!" (Surah Ghafir, Verse 16). While the wise man totally vanished, Haqq gives him a new being and a new life from His own being. This is the truth of certainty. The wise man is freed from the states of khawf and raja (fear and hope). This person becomes a successor of our Prophet. Whenever a person reaching this station says "Hu," he completely loses himself. He dies before dying.

Couplet:

Give the being to Haqq, may the being belong to Haqq Remove yourself and may the beloved remain so that you are safe

Couplet:

Anyone from all eternity was "hu" Anyone apparent and hidden was "hu"

If the person saying "Hu" has not matured and reached the stage of Annihilation in Allah by following a guide, he envisions Haqq based on his presumption. He worships a creator which he shaped based on his imagination. The verse "Have you seen ˹O Prophet˺ those who have taken their own desires as their god?.." (Surah al-Jathiyah, Verse 23) indicates this. This is very dangerous.

The heart of a servant is the treasure of Haqq. It should be cleared from anything but Haqq. Indeed, the hadiths say, "The heart of a true believer is the throne of Allah…" "The heart of a true believer is the treasure of Allah…" and "The heart of a true believer is the mirror of Allah…"

Haqq created this world and man as a mirror to Himself, and He presented His beauty to Himself on that mirror. He admired and fell in love with His own beauty by looking at it.

For example, if you place a couple of mirrors around a beautiful beloved,

that beloved would be seen differently on each mirror depending on the capability and talent of each mirror. Some would be curved, and some smooth. A wise man regards and acknowledges what he sees on each mirror is beautiful.

Couplet:

What is seen by hundred thousand eyes is apparent It is again Him, the demander of His beauty

A wise man says, "I haven't seen anything after which I didn't see Allah!" and another wise man says, "I haven't seen anything in which I didn't see Allah!" Another wise man says, "I haven't seen anything before which I didn't see Allah!" A mature wise man is who gathered and comprehended all these states.

Allah bestows marifa to those who attain the truth. Pursuant to the verse 35 of Surah an-Nur, "...Allah guides whoever He wills to His light..."

those who are guided first feel the smell of Haqq, hear His call, then see His beauty, and finally help those seeking Him to see. However, all these are possible in this world with heart. Such a person smells with the essence of his heart, hears with the ears of his heart, sees with the eyes of the hears, and he shows others by becoming the locus of manifestation. When Haqq approaches to His servant, that servant begins to smell the sweet odor of affinity. Then, the flashes of the light of existence shine in his eyes. This is called the state of marifa. When in this state, he sees some images and hears some voice from the magnificence of Haqq. It is difficult to bear them. These should definitely be experienced under the surveillance of a guide. When Hazrat Abd'ul Qadir Gilani was in this state, he saw a hand covering the whole sky.

At this point, the servant begins to pray saying, "My Lord! Allow me a blessed landing, for You are the best accommodator," (Surah al-Mu'minun, Verse 29). This landing is nothing but the station of trueness. At this station, grace and benevolence pour down on people according to their capabilities. Man rises from one stage to another. After passing the final stage, the seeker proceeds towards the realm of reunion. Only those who are very talented from the past-eternity may reach here.

LOVE is essential to reach Haqq. Once this occurs, man would pass beyond the mountains and plains with a few steps. The traveler of truth can only walk on this path with love.

Love is fire; it burns the hearts of the travelers of truth all the time. This fire may only be extinguished with the wine of love. This wine is offered in a glass of proximity by the cup bearers. The essence of the heart feels its taste.

Finally, the verse "...and their Lord will give them a purifying drink," (Surah Al-Insan, Verse 21) manifests and the wine of reunion is drinking from the hand of power of Haqq. Thus, the reunion with Haqq occurs. The traveler of truth finds what he seeks. The verse, "And if you looked around, you would see bliss and a vast kingdom..." (Surah al-Insan, Verse 20) occurs.

Only those who abandons their existence may attain this bliss. Because the compensation for the existence abandoned is Haqq.

Only those demanding Haqq may unite with Him. We will demand Him, but we shall not exceed the limits. Because the extreme demands would be unreciprocated.

Demand. If a path opens, walk. Otherwise, wait without insisting. But never be tired of waiting. Do not be insistent. Wait for the verse "...We will surely guide them along Our Way..." (Surah Al-Ankabut, Verse 69) to manifest. Then, proceed on your path with the beneficence notified in the verse "...those whose hearts Allah has opened to Islam, so they are enlightened by their Lord?..." (Surah az-Zumar, verse 22).

Make effort to strengthen your love and eagerness and pray a lot to be successful so that everything is removed from our hearts except for Allah. May your love for the world disappear. May you watch the door of your heart to avoid worldly things to enter in. (Remain in a state of avoidance.)

Our state may change from time to time. Do not worry about it. Proceed on your path. Proceed in all weathers. Never be upset thinking you are not talented! If you are resolved on the path of Haqq, it means you are talented. You won't seek this path unless you have the talent (capability).

Allah first tests a person, then He opens the path. Therefore, do not be hopeless. Supplicate and shed some tears. Ask for forgiveness for your mistakes.

The efforts of those who complain saying, "I tried so much, but I am not awarded!" would go down the drain. Even such a thought is a disaster. Allah forbids!

Continue until you receive the warrant in the verse "...Allah is pleased with them and they are pleased with Him..." (Surah al-Ma'idah, verse 119).

Make effort to be appreciated by Haqq, not the public. Make things that would please Him, because He suddenly pulls His servant toward Himself with an unexpected divine attraction pursuant to the verse "...Allah chooses for Himself whoever He wills..." (Surah ash-Shuraa, verse 13).

Do not anticipate something immediately after performing some worships and doing some charities. Be patient and wait for what will be appreciated. He is such a beautiful appreciator. He always responses to every effort of His servants. He gives His union to those who prefer Him and abandon the world. What did Yunus say? "What they call heaven is a couple of angles and a couple of houris; give them to those asking for them, I only ask for and need You."

When the attraction of Haqq begins to manifest in different creatures, the servant is pulled towards Haqq with an attraction.

One should be in difficulty to experience these. One who is not in difficulty may not supplicate. We are in need of Him in every deed and need. Pray Allah remembering that we are helpless. You should feel that your heart is enlightened as you proceed on the path of meaning.

Your sorrow ends when you empty your heart from everything except for Allah. You find peace. Because anything in your heart that is related to the world distresses you.

When Haqq comes to your heart, all your suffering ends. You would be one of the saints protected by Allah.

Allah is very compassionate and merciful towards people. Be hopeful of Allah, and wait for the gospel saying, "Haqq has certainly come to you from your Lord..." Because Allah does not fit into the earth or the skies. But He fits into the heart of a believing servant. You are that heart. You are a human with that heart.

Our Prophet said, "Leave your stomach empty, clean your outside, it is hoped that you see your Lord!" (...) Hazrat Ali said, "Allah is not seen with the eyes. Only the hearts see Him through the truth of belief!" (...) Hazrat Umar said, "My heart has seen my Lord!"

Our Prophet said, "The scent of the Most Compassionate comes from Yemen..." With these words, he implied that the scent of the Most Compassionate spread from Uwais al-Qaran. This tells us that the scent of the Most Compassionate spreads through the friends of Haqq. Those whose noses are opened to the meaning may feel this scent.

THE PERFECT MAN

All the living things in nature, plants, and animals physically mature.

Men mature in two ways: physical and spiritual. Physical maturing is the time-dependent growth. Spiritual maturing is independent of time. This is achieved independent from time after a certain physical maturing. It is related to the maturing of the conditions.

Those who accomplish their physical growth need to accomplish their spiritual maturing too. Otherwise, they would be immature. The immature things are tasteless. It is very difficult to tolerate immature people. They easily disturb and hurt people around them. They live distant from the reality. They are selfish and they do not care about others. They claim to be right about everything; they do not trust anyone; they only care about their own lives and look after their own interests. The meaning of life for them is only to eat, drink, get married and take pleasure. They consume their lives like this.

The end of being immature in this life is disappointment. Because we are planted on this land on the Earth to mature and give fruits. Not for falling on earth before maturing.

Our country and the world need mature people. The mature people are merciful and compassionate. They serve without expecting a reward. They do not bear grudge against or turn on anyone. They do not like discussing or fighting.

They believe that one day they would definitely die, and they will account for the evil they do in this world in the afterlife. After recovering from heedlessness and gaining consciousness in this world, they are cleansed and search for the truth with Haqq. They complete their lives according to the purpose of creation.

Man's purpose of creation is to know his Lord. He would only start to live a real life after that. He could see the essence of the objects and senses the truth. His inner ears hear and his inner eyes open. He switches to spiritual living from bodily living. His pleasures and feelings change. He eats, drinks, and sleeps enough to stay alive; and he sees the truth and depends to Haqq with his spirituality. Haqq sees and hears from him and Haqq speaks through him.

Thus, Haqq exhibits and notifies His attributes through him.

He truly lives with the qualities of Haqq. He perceives life differently. He would become the most honorable creature.

A person is born and grows up. He gets lost in heedlessness in a relentless struggle to achieve his worldly wishes and desires. He has busy schedules at every age. He gets older without thinking how the mighty have fallen. His life passes like this until he wakes up with a severe disease or an accident. When finally, he wakes up, it is too late.

This life that you see is not the true living; it is sustaining. It is feeding the body and allowing it to taste worldly pleasures. Living the truth is spiritual. Man can only live the truth with his spirit. One who is not aware of his spirit is unaware of Haqq. Yet, it is not possible to live truth without being aware of Haqq. The truth may only be seen with Haqq and lived with Haqq. The life has no meaning unless one looks, eats, or drinks for Haqq.

One who does not see the beauty of Haqq or who does not eat with Haqq does not truly live. He consumes his life in vain and only feeds his body. That body gets older and ruined one day. It returns to earth which is its origin. The spirit came from the Almighty Creator that is its homeland, and it return there. While some returns happy, others return in guilt and embarrassment. They pay for a life spent in vain. because our Creator created us to know Him. Knowing Him is only possible with Him. Attaining Him with Him is possible by finding nothingness. Wherever there is nothingness, Haqq fills it in.

We did not exist in reality. Our Almighty Creator provided us with a being out of His being. Do not forget that existence comes from Him and do not claim to exist. Remember that you do not exist in reality and give up this claim. Be aware that existence belongs to Haqq. Let's remove yourself and let our Creator remain.

Our Almighty Creator says:

"I was a hidden treasure and I wished to be known. I created mankind to be known. I made them love me so that they know me."

Only Haqq knows Himself truly. People only know Him with His actions and attributes.

Anyone seeking Haqq and the truth needs a guide. One may not seek Allah unless he loves Him. One may not love by himself. He needs a guide to make him love Allah. In this sense, our Prophet said:

"I swear on Allah who holds the life of Muhammed in His hands that the most valuable people before Allah are those who make people love Allah and Allah love people, and those who walk on the Earth by advising."

he wise teachers (murshids) open the mirrors of the hearts of those who depend on them. When the mirror of the heart purifies, divine lights reflect to that heart and the beauty of oneness becomes apparent. And these servants abandon worldly desires and wishes, and love and want Allah. Those whose inner eyes open know the reality of the world and the afterlife. They understand that the world is temporary. They do not care about the temporary and prefer the everlasting. Then, they try to completely follow the traditions of our Prophet.

Allah, the Almighty says:

"Say, o Prophet: "If you love Allah, then follow me; Allah will love you and forgive your sins. For Allah is All-Forgiving, Most Merciful," (Surah Ali 'Imran, Verse 31).

Our Prophet says: "People are sleeping. They need something to wake them up…"

In this regard, the first guide to us is our Prophet who was the servant and the messenger of Allah. He is the Perfect Man, and the best role model of perfection. Nobody has ever matured as much as he did.

How happy are those who meet and know him! Everyone typically finds him in their spiritual leaders. He may appear in any appearance. The truth of our Muhammed (pbuh) comes to a person in form of any man when that person is awake. When he comes, that person is respected in the same manner as our Prophet. They person is treated like our Prophet.

According to Abd'al Kareem Cili, the author of Insan Kamil (the Perfect Man), the person in whose image the Prophet of Allah appears is our Prophet's successor in the apparent world. And our Prophet is his truth in the hidden world.

The heart of the perfect man is the throne of Allah. Allah created him after Surah ar-Rahman. In that, Allah is alive, wise, powerful, disciple; He wills, hears all, sees all, and speaks all. And he is the same.

The perfect man has deserved the names and attributed which belong to the essence. He is the mirror of Haqq. His names and attributes are only seen in the perfect man. In this sense, Allah says, "Indeed, We offered the trust to the heavens and the earth and the mountains, but they all declined to bear it, being fearful of it. But humanity assumed it, for they are truly wrongful ʿto themselvesʾ and ignorant ʿof the consequencesʾ," (Surah al-Ahzab, Verse 72). Because as man is ignorant about his status, he tortured his ego and decreased his degree below his status.

The perfect man has a taste which is called "the taste of Godhead." He receives this taste from Allah and loses himself.

The perfect man sometimes peels off all these names and attributes, and he is not under the influence of any of them. At that moment, he is just one of the other people. He eats and drinks like them and lives a humane life.

In every century, Allah sent spiritual guides to show the true path to those who believe Him.

This hadith is an evidence to this:

Allah sends a person to this ummah to renew the religion at the beginning of each century.

The wise teachers are the guides of Allah. They are the friends of Allah. They guide those seeking Haqq. Our Prophet was guided by Gabriel.

The one seeking the truth may sometimes fail to understand the states he experiences and the dreams he sees. A guide would interpret them to him. The guide explains him what he must do. The most accurate way is for the guides to ask for and receive these explanations from Allah.

The number of people around a friend of Allah does not always show that he is a master of his domain. That person should have passed the stations of love and divine attraction and attained the reunion. Allah manifests in the hearts of such people.

Allah notified us about this reality as follows:

"Neither the earth or the sky nor my throne or my seat could take Me in. I could only fit into the heart of a believing, purified and cleansed servant."

"I would be his ears, eyes, tongue and hands. He hears with Me, sees with Me, speaks with Me and holds with Me."

The friends of Allah should have proceeded from the light of state to the light of Haqq. The light of Haqq relieves the intoxication by the light of state. A man of state may not have a disposal.

When those who took the friend of Allah as a guide repented and abode by him, they would have abode by our Prophet. If they abode by our Prophet, then they would have surrendered Allah. In this sense, Allah says in His Book:

"Surely those who pledge allegiance to you are actually pledging allegiance to Allah. Allah's Hand is over theirs. Whoever breaks their pledge, it will only be to their own loss. And whoever fulfills their pledge to Allah, He will grant them a great reward," (Surah al-Fath, Verse 10).

The friends of Allah fully benefit from the apparent and hidden knowledge and abilities granted to them by Allah, and they bring those who abide by him to Haqq by listening to Him. Allah evaluates and appreciates all these efforts. These guides cut all the negative worldly connections of the people that they are responsible for, prevent them make friends with harmful people, and determine and help them to get rid of their bad habits one by one. They show the good qualities and prepare basis to adopt the manners of Allah.

The friends of Allah literally follow the sharia of our Prophet. They provide treatment like doctors. They are capable of solving any social and economic problems. They test those who are abide by them in terms of loyalty and attachment as required so that they do not take pains for nothing. Because they will be trained as a diver to extract the pearl of truth from depths of the sea.

The friends of Allah do not discuss with anyone about their duties. They do not try to prove themselves. Because they assume these duties from Haqq through their masters.

You should not discuss or scold anyone before the friends of Allah because our Prophet didn't like such people.

You should not object to the friend of Allah, and you should exactly do as he recommends. You should not as for proof. Because asking for proof is lack of belief in the guide.

A seeker on this path only understands what he sees apparently. He is not aware of what is notified to the inner heart of the guide by Haqq. The traveler of this path is the one who is seeking Haqq. The guides teach them the rules of good manners.

The friends of Allah talk differently in every setting. They do not talk about the things that they discuss with wise men among public. They tell everyone to the extent one can understand.

Allah granted charismatic gifts to make His friends loved and respected, and to show His power. However, the friends of Allah refrain from attempting to show their charismatic gifts to show off intentionally.

When a seeker of Haqq sees a dream or experiences a state, he should not tell about this to anyone except for his guide. His guide should not make an explanation about this to him. But she should give useful advices.

Visiting other guides would harm the seeker of Haqq. The heart of the seeker blurs if it shifts towards the other guide. This is like a patient using the drugs prescribed by two different doctors.

The friends of Allah live by thinking that Allah looks into their hearts every moment and He is aware of their every state.

When they meet someone whose rank they do not know about, they do not consider themselves superiors. They treat their circle with compassion. They are very humble.

Visiting the friends of Allah with an intention to test them is ignorance.

If a person pursuing the path of truth under the guidance of a friend of Allah witnesses all kinds of spiritual disposals of his guide yet hesitates about his guide upon hearing or seeing anything negative, then he assumes his guide to be insufficient and he could not benefit from his guide.

The friends of Allah practice abstinence to enhance their manners. They endure the sufferings from Haqq, and they do not torture anyone. They bear the burden of the society. They help the helpless. They warn those who are unaware. They teach the ignorant. They do not refuse visitors. They host the guests without regarding them as burden. They show concern for and give confidence to those afraid. They feed the hungry and dress the naked. Because Allah has become their seeing eyes, hearing ears, speaking mouth, and holding hands.

They do not act according to their own wills. They do not have any wishes related to the world or the afterlife.

They stay away from what is forbidden and suspicious. They have disciplined their ego through bodily challenges such as hunger, thirst, and nakedness. In this respect, they died in four ways. These are white death with hunger; red death by abandoning desires and whims; black death by enduring the sufferings; and green death by wearing old clothes. They surrendered both worlds. They pursue only the consent of Allah in every deed. They preferred Haqq against public. They only ingratiate themselves with Haqq. They regard the places they visit to draw lessons.

They serve the society once they are freed from the evil of their ego. If a person starts doing these before being saved from his ego, satan will disgrace him. Satan makes him run after fame and reputation.

They are contented. They content themselves with what Allah appreciates for them. They do not set their eyes to more. They thank Allah in times of ease, and praise Allah in times of distress. They pray Allah to fulfill any need. Because everything is in Allah's power. They are terrified of objecting Haqq. They are hopeful of Allah in any matter.

They do not investigate anyone's defect or failure. They are occupied with theirs. They speak of good things when they talk, and they do not mention about the evil.

They are not lazy. They are avid and hard-working. They don't like unnecessary talk, and they only talk about good things. They never abstain from telling the truth to anyone. They reconcile the offended people in the best manner.

They have superior modesty. When they make a mistake, they are ashamed of Allah the most. They pray for the people and the societies; they are compassionate and merciful.

They make effort to remove anything agonizing people. They put the stone on the road aside.

They do not think that they have anything to claim from others; but they do the required to respond to and settle the claims of others from them.

They love those who love Allah. They do not like the enemies of Allah.

They do not lend money to anyone. If a needy asks for a loan, they give whatever they have without return.

When someone calls after them, they do not just turn their heads and look, but they turn with their whole body.

They do not believe in bad luck; they regard everything with good intentions. They are just and fair to their circle. They prefer the poor to the rich; they spend time with the poor.

This is the state of the friends of Allah.

Prophets and the friends of Allah are the representatives of Haqq in this world. The friends of Allah are the heirs of the Prophets; they are the scholars who know Allah.

They are aware of the good and evil thought coming to the hearts of people. They diagnose the behaviors from the ego and treat spiritual diseases. They understand from the smell of the people around them whether those people will improve or not.

It is not legitimate for a guide who is not qualified to train a seeker of Haqq to continue the duty; because he is like an inexperienced doctor causing his patient die due to malpractice. The seeker never hides anything from his guide; he believes that Allah will notify his guide of anything when required.

The friends of Allah who are guiding abstain from what is unlawful (haram); they are merciful towards people; they do not get angry or have grudge against the sinners; they love those who love Allah and stay away from those who Allah does not love; they order the good and forbid the evil; and they are not detained by anyone's disapproval.

They treat people with tolerance; they do charity; they remove anything agonizing people; they do not treat anyone unfairly; they are generous; they treat the senior like a father, the peers like a brother, the minors like a child, and they regard the entire humanity as their family;

they consider that the compliments and respect of the people come from Allah; they easily get on well with everyone; and they are mild-mannered people.

The compassion reflecting from Haqq is seen in their eyes. They are generally grieved. Although they seem to be in a state of joy arising from endeavor and enthusiasm, this does not actually arise from delight. They remind Allah to those who see them. Respecting the friend of Allah is respecting Haqq. However, the purpose of the seeker should be Haqq. When you meet the friend of Allah, all your problems end, and you feel a relief and peace inside. You heart fills with love. You don't want to leave him. You feel relieved, your eyes shine, and your face enlightens as you continue listening to his discourse. You unavoidably respect him.

The leader of the friends of Allah is our Prophet Hazrat Muhammed Mustafa (pbuh). He is Insan Kamil (the Perfect Man). He is the role model. Those who love him more than themselves want to be like him. He is our precious. May my Lord predestine us to visit him and gain his intercession (shafaat).

I love you more than my own existence
Seeing your beauty is my only intentness

My love turned into a fire
With you my dreams are delightful

I burnt with your longing
Your name gets me trembling

I wanted to come to you with my heart and soul
My heart left my body to knock your door

"Come," you said with your name Muhammed
You sent me off with your name Ahmed

Finally, I realized that I came to you from you
I put my face on the ground before you

As I raised my head from the ground
I lost my mind and turned crazy
Seeing before me, your beauty

You called out to me, "Do not bid farewell!"
You got on the bus taking us to Mecca

On the path of heijra in the desert
We heard a scream at the instant
A cloud was following us
Just above without leaving

O Muhammed!
You shed tears centuries ago
You missed your people and said hello

Today you showed mercy
And came to Kaaba with those who missed you

– Faruk Dilaver

KNOWING YOUR NAFS

The path of Sufism is the path of "truth." Those proceeding on this path become perfect men by imitating our Prophet. The attributes of our Almighty Creator manifest in them. Allah becomes their seeing eyes, hearing ears, and speaking mouths. For a person to reach this level, he should first know and discipline his nafs (ego).

The fact is that a person may know his Creator through knowing himself. Because it is ordained, "He who knows his nafs knows his Lord!"

The closest one to a person is again himself. He who does not know himself may not know others. Many people think that they know themselves, but this is not correct. Knowing oneself is not knowing your body, your height or weight; it is not eating a certain food when you get hungry or knowing your palatal delight; it is not your likes or dislikes.

Knowing yourself is possible through learning your reality. For this purpose, you need to find the answers to the questions such as "What are you? Why were you created? Where did you come from? Where will you go? What are you doing here?"

You did not come to this world to eat, drink, sleep, rest, get married and reproduce. Animals also do this. Different from them, you have intellect and judgment. You should think that you did not come to this world to fulfill the needs of your body which will eventually die and become earth.

Look at this worldly life; it is too short, and it passes so quickly! Immediately learn what you should do in this world before you eventually die.

To feel regret at the end will not provide you with another chance.

Man consists of a body and a spirit. Body is the visible physical structure and the internal organs of man. The spirit comes from Allah and it is invisible. It is the ruler of the lands of body.

Knowing Allah, observing His beauty is His attribute. It is a very precious ore. It will return to Allah at the end.

The spirit is the difference of dead and alive. The dead body does not have a spirit. The existence of the spirit is not felt.

Allah ordained our Prophet to notify the truth of the spirit as follows:

"And they ask you about the spirit. Tell them, 'The spirit is under the command of my Lord.'" He was not allowed to make further explanations.

The spirit is the essence of man. The whole body is dependent to it. Man is not this visible body. The majority of people perceive themselves as the body and live accordingly. They do not know their true identity. They are not aware of their spirit. Those who are not aware of their spirit are not aware of Allah nor they know Allah. Because Allah is known through the spirit.

Knowing Allah is possible by knowing the creatures of Allah. And that is the entire realm of creatures.

Body is the mount of the spirit. The spirit uses it. The spirit operates all its organs by commands.

"He who knows himself knows his Lord." In this sense, man himself is a mirror. Whoever looks at him sees Haqq. Unfortunately, many people look at themselves but fail to see Haqq. Whereas man should know the essence of Allah from his essence; the attributes of Allah from his attributes; the disposal of Allah in the universe from his disposal.

If man thinks of the essence of his body, he will see that he was created from a single cell. His body, with all his organs, was formed in his mother's womb by dividing and reproducing. How does that cell divide and get aligned to form this body? Could this happen all by itself? Or is there an Almighty Creator who creates it? Here, the own existence of man is an evident to the essence of Allah. Man did not occur by itself or by consequence. He has a creator. When the formation of man inside the womb is monitored and analyzed, one can't help being surprised how great is the power of the Almighty Creator. No one, except for the mighty Allah, may create such an incidence.

Man sees through the seeing attribute of Allah. He hears through the hearting attribute. He speaks through the speaking attribute. He knows through the knowing attribute. Man lives with the attributes of Allah. This is another secret of living. Who actually sees and hears through everyone?

O the seeker of truth, HAQQ is the bare truth. He eventually meets the one who is sincerely, earnestly, and persistently seeking Him.

Do not forget that the immortal may be found through death. You should die before death to find Him. The rich finds Him by being poor; you should be poor. The powerful finds Him by being helpless; then, you should be helpless. He bestows the truth and the true living to His servants like this. His being may only be found by disappearing. As you see, it is very easy to find Him, yet it is difficult to abandon existence and disappear. This is the whole point. You should perform the true prostration to disappear. This prostration requires hard work. Be determined to find Haqq. Your Lord would help you and make it easier. You should be hopeful of this. What did Yunus Emre say:

Finally, I knew myself; just so you know, I found Haqq
Until I found Him were my fears; now, I'm freed from my fears
I am not frightened anymore or concerned a little
Who shall I be afraid of now; whom I feared became my lover

Azrael does not come to me not the questioner to my grave
They have nothing to ask me, I became the one making them question
What can I be next to Him, how can I order His commands
He came in and my heart is full, I stood before Him

May lovers take from us, non-lovers never guess
No matter who takes or gives, I became an almighty shop
Haqq opened the door to Yunus, Yunus became the property of Haqq
Mine is the eternal power, I became the sultan when I was a servant

– Yunus Emre

You, too, should find someone who has already found, and follow his advices. Because Allah did not fit into the earth or sky, but He manifested in the heart of a person who has found. He was a hidden treasure, and He created the objects and spirits to be known. Open your eyes, look around you carefully. Know the Creator through His art and creating. Look and see that everything indicates Him with His art, just like the colors indicating light. Once you finish reading this book, read it once again carefully so that you attain its secret and become confidant with Haqq. You may not benefit from the information that you do not fully comprehend. Remember that the essence of Allah may not be seen with the bodily eyes in this realm. What is seen is the manifestations of His attributes.

Allah first created the spirit; the intellect failed to comprehend this. Then, He created the nafs. The indications of nafs are known in the world. Nafs is like the coordinator between the spirit and the body. It transmits what it takes from the spirit to body.

To know the nafs, one should know man. The face of Adam is the screen of his body. While creating him, Allah made angels build his body, and He made his face with His hand of power. Therefore, face has a deep meaning. According to the Sufi masters, "Head of a man is like the throne of the Most Compassionate. His face is a pure mirror reflecting the face of the Most Compassionate. The heart is like the seat. The inner heart is like the heaven. His breath is like the winds; his words resemble the thunder; his cry resembles the rain; his sorrow resembles dark clouds; his sleep resembles death; his dreams resemble the worldly life; his awakening resembles the resurrection on the Judgment Day. His childhood is like spring; his youth is like summer; his middle ages resemble fall; and his elder ages resemble winter."

Every nafs has the nature of an animal until it is disciplined. Some are cunning like a fox. Some are aggressive like a mad bull. Some are courageous like a lion. Some are peaceful like a lamb. Some are lonely like an owl. And some are hard-working like a bee.

Allah blew spirit into man from His spirit. The body of man is from earth and his spirit is from Allah.

Allah first manifests with His attributes in a beloved servant. Then, He gives His actions to His attributes.

People are connected to each other in two ways. The first one is the family connection, and the second one is the spiritual connection.

The important one is the relation arising from the spiritual connection. Because Allah said, "Believers are brothers and sisters!" So, warn your physical and spiritual brothers and sisters. Protect them from fire.

No matter what we learn or how well-informed we are, no matter how many spiritual experiences we have, never pursue becoming the head; be a foot if you can and run to serve. Because we already have a head; he is Hazrat Muhammed Mustafa. Live like him. Do not be assertive. Making an assertion is to claim something; and this is claiming to exist. You may not attain Haqq or the truth unless you abandon this state.

The path of truth is the truest and the most beautiful path of all. The seeker of truth reaches the purpose of creation and lives the reality by finding Haqq at the end of the path.

Allah sent Gabriel to our Prophet and wanted him to choose between being a Prophet who is a servant or a Prophet who is a sultan. In the meantime, Gabriel signed our Prophet. Upon this, our Prophet said, "I actually want to be a Prophet who is a servant!" It is understood from this incident that Gabriel had been the guide of our Prophet.

The heart of a man is the center of transportation and coordination in the body. Besides this biological function, it spiritually provides communication with unknown meanings. This is made with the inner eye. The inner eye only opens at the moment of death or sleep, and it sees what happened and what will happen in the realm of meaning to the extent allowed. This image is apparent as it is, or it is hidden that requires interpretation.

The Preserved Plate is where all that happened and will happen is written before the Almighty Creator. What is written there happens.

Heart and the Preserved Slate are like mirrors. When the heart turns towards the Preserved Slate, what is written on it reflects on the heart. For this, the heart needs to stay away from worldly feelings and emotions as well as being pure and clean. And this may only happen during sleep or at the moment of death. This is also possible in a state that is defined as dying before death; namely, being like a living dead. In such instances, the veil of heedlessness is removed from the heart.

"To die before death" is completely getting rid of the influence of worldly desires and wishes while living. If a person who reached such a state sits alone, closes his eyes, shuts down his feelings, cuts off his relationship with the world, turns towards Allah and says "Allah! Allah!" with his heart, then he may communicate with the realm of meaning. His inner eyes also opens while he is awake, and he feels like dreaming; and he can receive good images from the realm of meaning. He knows the unknown or accomplishes his spiritual training through these images and news. In this sense, Allah says, "We also showed Abraham the wonders of the heavens and the earth, so he would be sure in faith," (Surah al-An'am, Verse 75) and "remember the Name of your Lord, and devote yourself to Him wholeheartedly," (Surah al-Muzzammil, Verse 8). In such cases, the knowledge of Allah fills into the heart of man just like in Prophets. He knows his Lord through this knowledge; he watches the realm of angels and sees that they bring rain, descend snow, and shape babies in their mothers' womb upon the command of Allah.

Man's heart is also granted the power and ability granted to the angels. Thus, they dispose in the material realm. For instance, if his disposal orients towards a predatory animal, then that animal becomes dependent on him. If he sincerely prays for a patient, that patient recovers. If he wants someone to come to him, he makes that person come to him by influencing that person's meaning. He may do many other things, but these are not things an ordinary man can do. This requires dying before death. Prophets and saints are such people. The information that people may not attain even through reading come to their hearts. Such knowledge including the information related to the world of the unseen is called "Divine Knowledge." Regarding this matter Allah says, "There they found a servant of Ours, to whom We had granted mercy from Us and enlightened with knowledge of Our Own," (Surah al-Kahf, Verse 65).

Man can only reach the true happiness and attain the purpose of life by knowing the CREATOR. The happiness of lust is achieved by uniting with the partner; the happiness of rage is achieved by getting revenge from the enemy; and just like this, the happiness of the heart is achieved by knowing and loving Allah. A man without a happy heart may not truly be happy. The true life may not be lived unless the heart is satisfied with the desire of Allah.

Man knows the attributes of Allah through his attributes and he knows the essence of Allah through his own essence. One admires the might of Haqq through His work by looking at himself.

The heart is the truth of the spirit. And the spirit is from Allah. It came from Allah. Therefore, man knows Allah through his spirit. He sees and recognizes through his heart. One who attains his own truth unites with Haqq. Allah created Adam in His image. What is meant here is the truth of Adam. Namely, the spirit, the true identity.

CHAPTER THREE

INTERPRETATIONS OF YUNUS EMRE'S POEMS

THE TRUTH CREATED AN ORE

The Truth had an affection for Himself and an ore originated from this affection; he looked to that ore and the ore melted out of the glory of the Truth.

He created seven layers of earth from the light of that ore; He created seven layers of sky from the steam of that ore.

He created seven seas from the drop of that ore; He created mountain chains from the foam of those seas.

He created His Mohamed out of His compassion to the creatures; and He created Ali out of His compassion to the believers.

No one can know the unknown unless the Creator notifies them; these words are from the knowledge of Qur'an. Yunus got drunk upon drinking from that sea of ore as he thought about the wisdom behind that ore.

I LOVE YOU WITH ALL MY HEART

I love you with all my heart, I do not act upon customs, traditions, my path does not pass through this ceremony.

Just like the light is visible everywhere, on every being with its colors, you are also visible in every being wherever I look; you are everywhere. Where should I place you within me?

He is a beauty without qualification and has no description, He has no mark; how can there be a mark within the mark.

Do not ask me about myself, I am not myself. I gave up on me. My image walks empty within my clothes.

I cannot reach Him who took me away from me, who can reach, who can set foot within the sultan?

Some were predestined for manifestation; the Truth looked through their eyes, spoke through their mouths; some have intentions even beyond.

Whoever touched by the light of the beloved's sun, their lights become brighter than the Sun.

Your love has taken me away from myself; I consent to this suffering; such a suffering with a beauty within its remedy.

Religious laws are God's orders and prohibitions; religious orders are the path to maturate and reunite for those who fulfills them; truth and gnosis are even deeper.

They said Solomon knows bird language; how can Solomon know that language? There is a Solomon within Solomon.

I forgot everything, religion and piety got past me with love, what kind of a sect this love is, it is even deeper than the religion.

Those who give up on religion are in blasphemy. My Creator demonstrated Himself, I lost my faith; what kind of blasphemy is this even deeper than faith.

Yunus encountered the friend unexpectedly while he was on his way to the friend, he could not get through the door within him.

KNOWING YOUR ESSENCE

What is better than a person knowing his own essence, his own truth? Those who know their own essence are superior to others.

People should listen to advices and learn a lot; those who want to reach their ranges, intentions should beg in a soulful and sad state.

This path of spirituality is extremely far; its traps are earthly pleasures and desire. Those who get caught in one of these traps should not let their spiritual guides go.

Those who want to be sure of themselves on this path, who ask to be sure should stop speaking ill of any-thing and gossiping. If someone fails to see and under-stand correctly and leaves the true friend, he becomes destitute of reality and thinks he is right. If he sees the reality and becomes embarrassed one day, he should repent and put his face down on the floor by prostrating.

Those who serve to someone who is serving God will be freed from torment. Those who see the face of a true friend of God will definitely be forgiven.

Those who hear this news of Yunus will cheer up and rejoice. Those who want to reach to the treasure should follow the path of the friend of the Truth.

THOSE WHO COME TO THIS WORLD

Those who come to this world must be leaving eventually by taking their good and bad deeds together with them.

No one knows what death is like, it takes away people day and night. All children, husbands and wives will unhappily experience death.

Where are all the friends of God, the prophets? None stayed here, all passed by the Earth. The black earth has its mouth open and will swallow people one by one.

Those who spend their lives for gold and silver punish themselves. Tomorrow in the afterlife, whatever they collected will turn into scorpions and bite them.

Do not trust in your sibling, spouse, children, or friends. They cannot help you when death arrives. They will be desperate and can only stare into your eyes.

Oh Yunus! Remember the most Compassionate, let yourself get to the true friend. Do not keep feeding this body for nothing. The arrow of death will find you one day.

IF BOTH WORLDS BECOME A DUNGEON

Even if both worlds become a dungeon, they will be like gardens to me. There is no worry nor sadness for me because I met the true friend; the goodness comes to me from him.

Let me go the true friend and become his slave, let me bloom in the spirituality and become a rose. Let me also become the nightingale who sings for that rose; thus, my place will be in a rosary.

I saw the face of the true friend; I rubbed my face on the footsteps of the friends of God; these words of mine will be sweet like sugar to those who understand spirituality.

Those who give up from all cases and all claims do not get stuck anywhere; their hearts get wings and fly to the true friend. Those who drink the wine of love becomes both drunk and happy.

Without you, both worlds seem like a dungeon to me. Those who get to know Your love will become the best of the best.

My essence could not get enough of Your love, I am saying these words unintentionally and unaware. Yunus! These words of yours will become an epic for the people.

KNOWLEDGE IS TO KNOW THE KNOWLEDGE

Knowledge is to know the knowledge; knowledge is to know yourself. What is good of all the reading unless you know yourself.

What is the purpose of education? So that you know the Truth. It would be an effort in vain unless you become self-conscious.

Do not boast about your education or your knowledge! Do not trust in your worships! All would be efforts in vain unless you take the Sufi saint as the Truth, unless you consider the Sufi saint as the Truth.

The meaning of four Holy Books is hidden in an 'Alif. What's good of all the reading if you failed to attain the secret of 'Alif symbolizing unity and oneness despite all the reading.

Yunus says; o the scholar! No matter if you go to pilgrimage for thousand times. The superior of all worships would be entering in one's heart.

IF YOU ARE TRUE LOVER

If you are a true lover, then why do you claim to have reputation? If you are loyal to the path of the Truth, then why do you defraud through false assumption?

Unless you break all the idols in your heart, fraudulent are all your worships, unless you give up relying on worships, what God predestines?

Because now you have reputation, all your life become a fiction, let the one who knows the meaning tell us what is veiled and hidden.

Abandon the appearance, remove from yourself the name of existence, what is this image you have before your soul is prosperous?

Your eyes see; your ears hear, and you understand the issue and the meaning, sun lights the day, but what is this divine light through the night shining?

People pass away day after day; your neighbors will leave when the time is right for them. Death swallows all one by one, then what makes you an arrogant one?

Come closer if you are a true believer; watch the noteworthy stars created and praise the Sufi saints with me, stop defaming those who love God so that the denier become apparent.

The one who follows the orders here has his work done in the afterlife, if asked for an example, tell who is Hallaj Mansoor?

Yunus now speak so that God became the cupbearer to offer you wine, erase the doubt in your heart, what is the Trumpet blown on the Judgement Day.

O LIFE, YOU DECEIVED ME

O life! I trusted you to be endless, but you deceived me, what shall I do with you? You ended and made me immovable, o life, what shall I do with you?

You were my only sorrow and worry. You used to enliven me. You were my only purpose and the sultan of my heart. O life, what shall I do with you?

Everyone comes to leave; all worldly affairs are a lie. At the end, whoever reaches the end cry, o life, what shall I do with you?

Two angels on my left and right scribe my charities and evils. As my life runs out, the rope around my neck thins and breaks. Then, my life ends, the beauty of my face spoils. O life, what shall I do with you?

At least do not run away and leave me alone. Do not set me adrift. If, at all possible, do not drink the wine of death and drain away. O life, what shall I do with you?

One day, I will be left without you. I will fall prey to warms and birds. I will decay and become soil. O life, what shall I do with you?

Poor Yunus, don't you know about this fact? Don't you analyze and understand? Why don't you draw lessons from the ones who passed away? O life, what shall I do with you?

THE MAN OF LOVE, OPEN YOUR EYES

O the man of love, open your eyes! Have a look at the thought-proving Earth. See the beautiful flowers that come with blossoms, all leave after growing pale and falling off.

They blossom just like that, elongate to reach the true friend, just ask them for once, dear brother, where they are heading out for.

Each flower praises God with thousand appeals and supplications, all the birds remember that sultan with their pleasant voice.

They praise His might to realize everything every moment. They grow pale when they remember how short their lives are.

The colors of the flowers change day by day; they fall on the ground again. This is a life lesson if you understand. This is a life lesson which wise men understand.

Neither coming is endless not laughing is continuous. The bottom line is death, and it arrives. This life is spent in vain unless you hear about love.

If only you heard each word or you endured this sorrow; if only you pined away… so that you leave profit and loss behind.

You already know, everyone will come to pass; you already know, no one stays here forever; those who understand the true meaning of this will drink the juice of love.

Yunus keep these words in some place. Attain their meaning and be freed from yourself. Tell me if anything comes from you because all the good and evil come from God.

THE ONE KNOWING THE ORIGIN OF THE WORDS

O the one who knows the origin of the words, listen! Look, where all these words come from, do they seem to be mine? Those who fail to understand the essence of the words think that those are my words.

There are words that ease anxiety and give joy. There are words that drive a wedge between people and make them strangers. Both the honoring and disdain come to people through words.

The words do not come from black or white; they do not come through literacy or knowledge, they do not come from those people walking around, they all come from the calling of the Creator.

I've never attended to school; the wisdom in me is from the being o God. Even a hundred thousand soothsayers wouldn't know the meaning of my words. This destiny of mine comes neither from the signs of stars.

We don't receive light from the moon, but the Sun. Being a true man of love is not inherited from the family but attained on the path. Neither our livelihood nor our food comes from this house. They come to us from God, from God's ocean.

We are just a means in-between; we speak whatever comes to our heart. Because God orders us to tell, the wisdom comes from Him to this spirit.

Yunus! Sigh in grief, this world is a place to suffer. No one could be at ease, for relief comes from a sigh and a cry.

SACRIFICING YOURSELF FOR LOVE

Can he be a true lover without sacrificing himself for love? Can he be a true lover without making effort to reach the true friend?

Can he be a true lover without loving the true friend more than himself and without abandoning his desires and whishes despite the abundant pleasure and enthusiasm he has.

Love does not need proof; love is not disclosed or makes the rounds; a soul that is not in love do not ascend the skies. Can he be true lover without burning with the fire of love and abandoning itself to fire like the dragonfly?

Can he be a true lover without abandoning the desires and wishes of the ego; drinking from the glass of love; melting away with the discourses of the true friend; walking decisively on the path of the true friend without getting caught by causes and excuses?

Can he be a true lover without worshiping night and day; sharing the same state with the true friend in seclusion; and without burning during the discourses by leaning his head to one side?

Yunus, now, endure the hardship coming from the true friend! The true friend means no harm to you, he only wishes the best for you and he gives you suffering to make you a mature lover. Abandon negative thoughts!

THE ONE DIVING INTO THE SEA OF LOVE

Those who dive into this sea of love do not need a craft. Where else we may find such a sweet discourse and such a nice moment?

Do not worry for not having worldly goods or wealth. If you love the Beloved, ease the worry within your heart.

If you had ever seen the Beloved that I love, you would have sacrificed yourself even before hearing this advice.

The lover would not take advice, because he does not know advice. He has forgotten about arrogance and grudge, and he abandons worldly exchanges.

True lovers have a sign on their faces, they shed tears day and night and they always have bloody eyes. Everybody pursues religion and belief, but I swear religion and belief take you nowhere without love.

Everybody likes this religion and faith; I swear to God, religion and faith are pointless without love.

Yunus! Do not be arrogant, be humble among the lovers. Do not be mistaken by the spiritual states you experience. Put your head on their sill, sacrifice thousand lives for the sake of love, so that you find God.

GRASP LOVE

One should grasp love and never let it go in order not to be deprived at the end of this life. If you learn one letter of love, if you know the first letter of love that is 'alif', then you do not need to ask any questions to anyone.

If you hear what love says, if you follow love sincerely, if your only purpose is love, and if you live within love, you should sacrifice your life for love, you should consume your life for love; you may not sacrifice goods for love.

The sign of the wise men is that they are present in every heart; surrender yourself to them. Do not care about the gossips or criticism; do whatever they tell you, they do not speak meaningless words.

Don't you draw a lesson from the bees? They make honey from every flower. Likewise, the wise men walk from one heart to another and seclude. Neither a fly nor a dragon fly has honey in their holes.

If you want to hear words like pearls and jewels, and to experience their meaning, serve the wise men. Even if an ignorant man has knowledge and says thousand words, they are all meaningless; those words would not have an influence or effect on you.

Humble Yunus, the poison that kills man becomes an antidote in the hands of love! The bitter words spoken with love would not break hearts; the worships are performed with love; otherwise, they would not be legitimate without love.

TELLING WHAT ONE DESERVES

The best is not to tell what one deserves. Telling what is deserved is to admonish that person the face. This darkens and rusts the hearts.

If you want to remove the dirt and rust from the hearts, say such a word that is the most effective and the best of all.

God ordered you to speak the truth; those who are lying today will be embarrassed tomorrow in the afterlife.

Those who fail to regard every creature in the same way are rebels even if they seem like saints before the religious law.

Listen, let me tell you about the religious law and the truth: religious law is a vessel, and the truth is the sea.

The sturdier the wood of that vessel is, the more resistant it is to the waves of that sea.

O friend let me tell you something even deeper than my previous words! The infidel of the truth is the saint of the religious law. In other words, the one who hears and sees the Truth in reality, finds the proof and loses his faith. The Truth is no more invisible and unknown to him. Such a person is defined as a saint in the religious law.

We are the seekers of knowledge and we read the book of love. Our Creator is our teacher, and love is the university providing that education.

Ever since the friend of God looked deep into Yunus, everything happened because of that look.

The sturdier the wood of that vessel is, the more resistant it is to the waves of that sea.

I WALK BURNING

I am a lonely nightingale walking around in this garden of life by burning; my chest is stained with blook by the thorn of the rose, and I am wandering around helplessly. I am neither wise nor mad; I am simply confused. Come and see what love has done to me.

I sometimes blow like winds, sometimes go off like the roads, and I sometimes overflow like floods. Come and see what love has done to me.

I gush out like rivers with the vigor of love. I tear my sorrowful heart down with the fire of love. I cry as I remember my dear wherever I wander around. Come and see what love has done to me.

Hold my hand, raise me, and prepare me, or allow me to meet and join you. You made me cry a lot, rejoice me. Come and see what love has done to me.

I travel from one city to another. I talk about the true friend with everyone. Nobody knows how I am, nor they recognize me in foreign lands. Come and see what love has done to me.

I am searching for and dream about my beloved like Majnun; when I wake up and realize that it is a dream, I become downhearted. Come and see what love has done to me.

Humble Yunus, I am helpless, I am in wounds from head to toe because of love. I am far away from the land of the true friend. Come and see what love has done to me.

I AM NOT HERE TO STAY

I am not in this world to stay forever; I will live for some time and leave when I consume my life. I searched for the truth in this world, and I found it. Now, I am here to sell it to whoever wants to buy.

I did not come here for my personal issues; my job is to love. The house of the true friend is the hearts. So, I came to prepare those hearts for the Truth to enter in.

This madness of mine comes from the intoxication by the true friend. A lover would know about the state I am in. I abandoned duality, and I came to disappear upon reaching unity.

He is the Sultan, and I am His servant; I am the nightingale of that garden of the true friend. I came to rejoice and sing in the garden of my teacher.

Those who do not know each other in this world may not recognize each other in the hereafter. I came to know the true friend and tell him about my state.

Yunus says, "I fell in love and died because of my yearning for the beloved. I came here to serve for and consume my life for the man of love."

YOUR LOVE TOOK ME AWAY

Your love took me away and made me forget about myself. There is only you on my mind and in my heart. I am burning with your longing every day; all I want and wish for is you.

I will not be happy with wealth or property, nor will I feel depressed because of poverty. I will only rejoice and console with your love; all I want and wish for is you.

Your love makes the lovers abandon all the wealth and desires; detaches the lovers from their own selves and makes them die before death. Just like a drop that falls into the sea and becomes the sea once they unite, your love embellishes me with all kinds of reflections from you and fills me up with manifestations. All I want and wish for is you.

Let me burn upon drinking the wine of love by losing myself in the words and eyes of the true friend. Let me climb the mountains out of his longing. You are my only thought during the day and night. All I want and wish for is you.

Sufis need discourse. Ahis need the afterlife. Majnuns need Layla. All I want and wish for is you.

Yunus is my name, and the fire of love within me increases day by day. My only wish in two worlds is you. All I want and wish for is you.

THE ONE WHO REPROVES ME

O, the one who reproves and condemns me because I am in love! If you are strong enough, come and save me from love; or else do not speak evil against me if you are not able to save me.

No one switched from state to state willingly; the lover assumes that he lives what he desires to; but even that desire comes with a state, the Almighty One determines and predestines the states of all of us. If you entered in a state with love, and if you experienced something under the influence of that state, and when you come to your senses after that state ends, do not regret what you have experienced and speak bad words, because God predestines those experienced with love.

All the states of the lovers are predestined by the Beloved; if you regret what you have experienced and have anything to say, go and tell Him. I must live the state given me by the Beloved. There is nothing I can do!

Whoever had a sip from the glass of love; a stranger, a friend, or a drunk are the same to him.

Whoever took the veil off the true friend's face lived was real; there are no more veils for him, neither goodness nor evil.

I am afraid to tell out of my respect to religious laws; otherwise, I would have given you detailed information about love. If I were to tell the details of love, I am afraid there might be points contrary to religious laws. In fact, there are no contradictions, but there are secret exceptions specific to lovers. These may be contrary to religious laws in appearance due to decency, but they are proper in terms of meaning.

If Yunus is killed with the sword of the true friend, if he dies upon the verdict of the true friend, he will not be upset. The star that sets in the sky of the true friend, rises again in the tower of the Beloved.

WHOEVER NEEDS A TRUE FRIEND

Let me tell what the one searching for a true friend should do; he shall first abandon his own self and never mention about what he was again.

The tradition of lovers is to give up everything they have and to sacrifice themselves for the sake of the true friend. All lovers consider being killed by love as a gain.

No one can be free from tricks and deceits without falling in love. Love saves everyone from the trouble of world and the afterlife.

Not every soul deserves being wasted on the path of the true friend without involving unrest, envy, and hypocrisy; otherwise, all loves hope to be sacrificed for the true friend.

The one going toward the true friend should abandon his own self; all his wealth and value judgments; then the true friend takes the fortress of heart and ransacks the city of soul.

There is no turning back from the path of the true friend once you head towards that path; don't you see that everyone will pass away, and no one will be immortal? Once you enter in, the best thing is to walk on the path of the true friend until death and never turn back. Those who escape from the true friend without being patient or upon seeing some behaviors that they consider as irrational or contrary to their value judgments and interests will be abstained from this purpose.

The bodily eyes may not see where the assembly of the true friend is. It is the inner ears that hear the divine songs of these lovers.

Yunus never loved anybody in this world but the true friend. Don't you know that everyone laughs at that one who fail to make effort to walk on the path of the true friend.

IF YOU SEE THE WAY I DO

Anyone who sees the face of his beloved like I did would become mad and climb the mountains; he may not endure, and he abandons his very self.

Which one of the beauties that I saw on your face could I tell! It is the lips of my soul that feels the beloved's fatal tang.

Wherever and whichever country my pretty charming beloved goes, impresses, and influences the severity two nations.

A person talks about whatever he loves, so I cannot help speaking his words all the time.

No one is worthy for the true friend by themselves, willingly or by making effort. Although this path requires effort, it requires a grace from God. The Almighty Creator places the star of the lover of His choice on top of the tower of affinity.

My words are like an echo from a rock to those who have no troubles or worries. Speak to yourself, hear yourself; those who experience the same state would know the hidden secrets in the other's heart.

If Venus had seen what this Yunus saw, she would have put aside her instrument, descended and pursued the beauties I had seen.

EVER SINCE I LOVED YOU

O, the true friend! I have lost my mind ever since I loved you; you are always in my heart and I am living you all the time. I lost myself in the Truth by reaching the sea like the rivers.

If a particle of love's fire falls into the sea, it boils the seas. I fell into the fire of love, and yearned and burned.

If there is love in a heart, that heart would not think of and worry about anything else. Ever since I lost myself in this love, I have been freed from all worries and I began to smile all the time.

The nightingale had also fell in love with the face of the red rose. I saw the face of the Sufi saints and began to write epics of love.

You have given me this love, what shall I do with my own self? I am full of divine light inside and outside; I fell in love with the true friend.

I was a deadwood dropped down on the road. One of those who attained the Truth looked at me with a beam, and I became a young boy.

Yunus, if you are a true lover, name yourself the humble! I abandoned all my wishes and desires; I found nothingness.

YOU ARE MY DEAREST

You are my dearest, I may not even make one step or speak a single word without you my only purpose is to reach you and to be with you. If I am not going to be with you in the heaven, I swear to God I do not want such a heaven!

Wherever I look, I see you. Because you are clearly evident. You are everywhere and on every item like the light; you appear with your colors and attributes. If I speak, you are my words, what else can I speak of? I am always talking about you everywhere and on every occasion. I do not have any wish except to watch you and to find a trace of you.

Yunus is also burning, he fell in love with you. Please show him your face! You are my one and only beloved; there is no one else other than you.

HERALD THE LOVERS

Herald the lovers, this love becomes a great power; whichever soul the love touches, it lefts a sign from its own soul.

If he abandons all his loved ones except for God and if he does not let his heart skip to anyone else, then whatever he watches all the time is both the essence and the attribute.

Those who are capable of anything, who set their hearts on God, who see the true friend eye to eye abandon all the creatures.

The love Yunus mentions lasts forever, it has no ending, and everyone admires it.

YOU ARE CLOSER TO US THAN OURSELVES

You are closer to us than ourselves; but you may not be seen because of your veils! If you want, you may be seen; but why do not you appear. Is there any fault in being seen; what is that beautiful veil covering your face?

You know such affairs, who and what to give, from whom and what to take. It is you to give and take. Only you know what and why to do something? Then, what is this call to account?

Where is the sultan of this property? If it is this body, where is its soul? I wish to see him, then why is mourning for the deceased?

Yunus, these physical eyes do not see him! There are those who see with their inner eyes, but they do not tell that they see. This delicacy is beyond comprehension. What is this deceit about?

I WALK ALONG THIS PATH

I have been walking along this path; I encountered several trees which grew exceedingly long; they are so nice and pretty, that my heart tells me to open some secrets.

What is the meaning of growing that long; as this world is mortal. This is the sign of arrogance, come closer and prefer being humble.

You nicely embellish yourself and wear pretty cloths. Reach out to the Truth with your heart, what else do you want, what else do you need.

The tree dries, the wheel turns, the bird lands on a branch for once. No bird has landed on you yet, neither a pigeon nor another bird.

Yunus, now see all your deficiencies! When you ask the directions to a deadwood, switch to the true path by realizing the wisdom.

LISTEN TO ME EVERYONE

Listen to me everyone, the elder and the young ones, I have news for you! I am a very happy man because I have a beloved like him.

If I am walking, it is to search for you; if I am speaking, it is to talk about you; if I am sitting, I am with you; who else would I need?

I no longer walk, seek nor travel long distances to find that the true friend because I found the true friend within me. I do not have another expedition.

The merchants travel long distances to purchase goods and make profit. Yet, I have the ore within myself; I do not need to purchase or sell.

Ever since the soul of this poor Yunus reached the true friend, his love continues to increase day by day because it was deemed as such from a glorious station.

NEVER SET YOUR HEART ON THE WORLD

Never set your heart on or tend towards worldly pleasures one day! Those who set their hearts on this world fall into the traps of interest and lust by being gravitated by it one day.

This world is an absorber, it absorbs the realms. When death arrives, it takes our body and absorbs it one day.

See this truth, my brother, many lie in their graves mixed with soil. Earth takes us into its arms just like them one day.

If man were prepared to leave this house of body like a falcon, he would abandon that body and fly to God like an arrow from the bow one day.

Poor and helpless Yunus! Never trust in what you see and know; pursue the Sufi saints and walk along their path. Flow to the sea like the rivers to reach God one day.

THE ONE WHO CLAIMS TO BE IN LOVE

The one who claims to be in love should be free of greed and whim; those who enter the house of love should avoid from walking away from the Beloved for a passing whim by inclining toward pleasure.

Expecting dignity and honoring is love for world. Anyone who fancies worldly reputation should not mention about love. A true lover no more talks about the world or the afterlife; a lover does not make a step for dignity or honoring.

Those who only speak about love do not know what love is. Those who fancy the dignity and honoring of this world shall not be called lovers; otherwise, it would be a slander.

Whoever has love has nothing left in him. He may not reach the beloved if his mount is a horse, mule, or a camel.

They should not aspire by calling Yunus a lover; many regretted and gave up the long distance they would take.

LOOK INTO MY HEART

O, the beloved! Take a look at my heart, what's inside? There are people who thing that this state of love we have is funny and who laugh at us finding it strange.

Let be! May the Truth be ours; that is enough for us. Never be upset by their laughter; they are in heedlessness! How can they know that there are many meanings in our attitudes and behaviors arising from loving God this much.

This path of love is long, it has many targets to reach, and it is difficult to proceed. This road does not give free passage; there is yearning for being apart, and there are tests.

Whoever is a brave lover, come to light to show your talents so that we see who has the ability!

Yunus do not come to light here, or you will be embarrassed! There are numerous brave lovers on the stage.

MY EYES AND MY HEART

My eyes and my heart are filled with love; my tongue speaks about my beloved; and my face is wet with my tears.

My body burns with love like a firebush; my smoke disperses, and it is the morning wind for those who see.

The armors made of iron may not bear this fire of love; the arrow of love stings the soul; this is the method; this is its way.

I mention about my king in my way; my king speaks to me; he is with me all the time; he is coming to me every moment.

Those who love you don't have sense! Even if they have a clear head for a moment, they are away from their senses any moment; they are crazy with love.

Yunus! You'd better be the soil on the path of Sufi saints; they became the Truth with the Truth. The range of the Sufi saints is greater than the throne.

O FRIENDS, O BROTHERS

O, friends! O, brothers! I'm afraid of dying one day. I am actually concerned about suffering for my mistakes and sins rather than being dead.

One day, all my actions are revealed to me; my sins and failures are told to my face; I am off my head being concerned about what to do and how to account for.

If I had been a true servant, I would have fulfilled my Lord's orders and been His servant; I would have burned and yearned for Him rather than being lost in worldly pleasures so that I rejoice in the afterlife.

I came to this world; I was seized by the wishes and desires of my ego and I became its slave. I failed to worship properly and do a lot of charity so that I am saved from that torture.

O, poor and helpless Yunus! He has lots of sins, what can he do! I took refuge in my God; I rely on His mercy to be forgiven.

THE POOR MANKIND

The miserable and poor mankind remained incapable and weak against the wishes and desires of the ego. They ate and drank just as they wished like animals and beasts, and they lost themselves in lust and pleasure.

They are not aware that they can die anytime, and they do not mention about the day they will die. They are heedless because of worldly occupations and heedlessness took their minds away.

The youngsters do not benefit from advice; the brave ones do not regret and repent for their mistakes; the elder ones are still heedless, and they fail to pray, life has gone like the wind and it won't come back.

The rich ones have gone too far and derailed, and they have forgotten about the poor. They get out of the sea of mercy and followed their egos by getting lost in pleasure.

Yunus! Listen the wise men, sit down with the wise men; and stay away from cruel people. Be afraid that you will die one day because all people who were born died.

ASK THOSE WHO KNOW

Those who know should be asked about this soul. Soul is the might of God, then what is the blood?

Idea is a servant; man serves with his ideas. Worry is the blood of fear and sorrow that feeds them. These sighs are the cloths of love; love is dressed in them. Who is the Sultan sitting on the throne of the heart?

Praise be to His unity that He created us from Himself when we did not exist. Actually, we do not exist. He is the only one to exist. What is all the property for a non-existing one?

God created us so that we can see the world. This world was not left for King Solomon; so, it is not eternal for anyone.

Ask Yunus of Tapduk, ask Yunus whose heart is always with Tapduk, what did he understand from this world? This world has no end, all those come leave; he will also leave one day, then why is this discrimination?

SUFFERING AND HARDSHIP COME FROM YOU

O the Beloved! Both the suffering and hardship come from you. How may I not sigh or cry! I fell into the fire of love; how may I not burn and yearn?

Here I am walking around in fire with your love; my desperate grief for you consumed me. I became crazy for you; how may I lie down to sleep?

May I fall into and get lost in the sea of your love like a drop. I do not have anyone else other than you to hold my hand. Do not abandon me so that I am not perished and ruined.

If all the beauties of eight heavens get together and they are offered to me, they may not keep your place, I may not prefer them to you.

Yunus Emre! Even if you repeat these words a thousand times to praise Him, they are still insufficient. Those who hear your words already fall in love with you; so, I would better cut the long story short.

GOD WILL SEND TO YOU

God will send the officer to take the soul one day. He will come and appear before you and make your face pale.

He will say: "The One who has given you that life temporarily wants it back," and he will do his final struggle with you.

He will take that life away from you, leaving your body empty and dry. Your sins will be hung around your neck and your ego will cry.

Your relatives will share your properties; they will transfer you there and you will see your grave when you go into the pit.

They will put you into the grave and say that your place is blessed. They will throw soil and stone from the Earth to cover you in a hurry.

You will be in a dark place, left alone with your deeds, you will then sigh and play the instrument of final regret.

Yunus, now come to repent. Perform worships and do charities while you are still alive. Come with love and put on this belt of dervishhood to become a seeker of the truth.

I WAS WALKING TO REFRESH

I was walking around in the morning to refresh when I saw the graves in the cemetery. I saw those which were once delicate bodies mixed in mother earth.

The body was decayed in the soil and lying secretly in the grave; I saw blood drained from the vessels, and shroud stained with blood.

I saw graves ruined, filled with dust, became indistinct, I saw many exemplary situations of those who are now away from all the worries.

I saw people who might no longer go to highlands to spend the summer or quarters to spend the winter. I saw mouths and tongues which might not tell about their states although they were crushed under earth.

Some of them pursued pleasure, some of them went out to bars, some of them were in trouble… I saw days turned into nights in the graves.

I saw dimmed black eyes, I saw indefinable pretty faces and I saw hands which once picked roses under the mother earth.

Some of them were lying with submission, some of them surrendered their bodies to earth, and I saw some who were offended by their mothers and bent their heads.

Some of them were crying and flailing around when the demons of hell burned their souls with fire; I saw smoke from the graves on fire.

Where did Yunus see it all and how he made us know? I am taken aback for seeing those.

SINCE I DIVED INTO YOUR WISDOM

O, my Lord with endless power! Since I dived into your wisdom, I am unaware of myself. I counted your qualities but could not get a grasp of your secret.

Your face cannot be described with words, no one knows the true you and your might, I could not be worthy enough to tell.

You are the first and the last; you are present everywhere, there is nowhere without you; why could I not see you.

It drove me mad not being able to see you, and sometimes I made mistakes and committed sins; I lost my mind with your love, I cannot get sober from this drunkenness.

You enraptured me by giving me life and a heart; do not take me apart from you, I rejoined, I cannot draw apart.

You gave me the life, told Azrael to take it, I got this life from you, I cannot give it to anyone else. You are the origin of my life, my life came from you, and it will return to you. No means needed between us, my life voluntarily rejoined you before death; it again wants to come to you unforced, voluntarily.

O the Creator of Yunus! Remove the curtain in between now. Let me see your beauty, I am loyal to your path, I cannot act upon lies.

THE SPIRITUAL WORLD CAME TO MY HEART

The love of the spiritual world came to my heart again, Haqq's country, my real homeland; let me go there, calling out to the true friend. Whoever go there stay there; let me also stay, calling out to the true friend.

Azrael comes and holds onto my life, cries of my mother and father do not help, he would not leave me to stay, I will get on that wooden coffin; let me go, calling out to the true friend.

Let me be busy in seclusions, remembering my Lord in desolate corners, a rose blossoming with his love, a nightingale in the garden of the true friend; let me go calling out to the true friend.

They make a cerement for my body out of this few meters' long cloth; let me make this earthly dress and sing calling out to the true friend.

Like Majnun who went wandering in deserts, let me perish with the love of my God. Let me cross high mountains, be a candle to burn and melt longing for the true friend, calling out to the true friend.

Days pass by years turn around; life comes to an end; soil is poured on me; my skin decomposes and becomes soil; let me dust calling out to the true friend.

Yunus Emre go down your path, non-believers do not go down that path; let me be a duck and dive to the lake of the true friend calling out to the true friend.

FRIENDS OF GOD CAME WITH LOVE

Even if the friends of God who come with love suffer and drink poison they still do not curse or speak bitter words. They always speak beautiful and sweet words, turning poison into honey. Inexperienced lovers who got their shares of love a little challenge friends of God who dived into seas of love and compare themselves with them.

On this path, we neither got sick and tired of listening to discourses of friends of God nor became too lazy to go to them. We went to them with sincerity. We did not become hypocritical or trickster by getting familiar and blind out of closeness. We did not put ourselves in doubt and tried to run away by searching for mistakes and flaws in the acts of the true friend. Everybody faces consequences of their own actions.

We talked hypocrite and trickster babblers off and showed their true faces. Those who see their dark faces without any divine light are as if they see a wild monster and push them away.

We do not need those who come to this discourse but do not get its taste, those who do not get the smell of the breath of the Truth, those who do not see the face of the Truth and assume people do everything, those who want but also deny the Truth. Send them away, let them go; if they stay, they cause trouble and set people against each other.

Those who are ignorant do not understand from spirituality, they do not think they will die and make nice decisions; they argue and fight with everybody as if they will never die.

No matter how high egos get with their desires and wishes and seem impassable like mountains, a way can be found to cross them. My Yunus Emre shows the way to those without a path, help them become more beautiful and better.

DO NOT SETTLE FOR A LOOK

Let us not settle only for a look, let us go to the true friend, my heart. Let us not die with longing, let us go to the true friend, my heart.

Let us go before the life ends, before it prepares to leave the body, before an enemy gets in between and misguides, let us go to the true friend, my heart.

Let us go, do not stay afar, make preparations for the true friend. The stop is on our guide's level, let us go to the true friend, my heart.

Let us leave our home, our city, cry out for the true friend, capture our beloved, let us go to the true friend, my heart.

Let us not stay in this world, it is temporary let us not be deceived, let us not get separated while we are one, let us go to the true friend, my heart.

Let us pass away from this world, fly to the land of the true friend, give up all desires, let us go to the true friend, my heart.

Come, be my guide, let us change our direction towards the true friend, let us not think about the past or the future, let us go to the true friend, my heart.

This world will not last forever, open your eyes to the truths, warn yourself; come, be a companion and a fellow to me, let us go to the true friend, my heart.

Before the end is disclosed, the death lays its hands on us, Azrael makes his move, let us go to the true friend, my heart.

Let us rejoin with the true friend of God, ask him of news about the Truth, take Yunus Emre with us, let us go to the true friend, my heart.

I CAME TO THIS WORLD ALONE

I got a body and came to this world from the spiritual one in a poor state, I will get tired of this world. I am trapped inside this body, when the time comes, I will get myself freed from this captivity.

I left the true friend and came here, I searched and found that beloved here; I was hanged like Mansur Al-Hallaj, burned, I will become ashes and dust away.

As I read the book of love, I studied and was educated in love; I do not write on black but on white.

The meaning of the four books is hidden in an 'alif; do not make me tell everything, if I do maybe I go off this path.

Let us not say bitter or sweet to any water coming out of a fountain, it is a shame for us to vilify, I leak out of a pipe. To vilify a discourse saying it is good or bad is not appropriate. So, I tell the secrets coming from within me sensibly.

I am being blamed because I said all seventy-two groups of people are right. I am afraid for the non-believers; otherwise, I would not be sad or angry!

How can inexperienced followers of the religious law show us the way? I became a duck and swam in the sea of the truth, I dived in and out of the realities.

The true friend told me to go to him, he remembered me, and did not forget; with all our crimes, I deem this invitation holy.

Yunus! This is the language of the birds; Prophet Solomon knows this; I sense whatever a real lover does on this path.

LISTEN, THE ONE ASKING OF ME

Those who are asking what I am! Listen, let me tell you the story of my existence: My image was created out of water, earth, fire, and air.

Like building four walls out of four opposite objects earth, water, air, and fire; came to exist my body as a miracle.

He kept earth hanging in air with wind, stored fire safely inside water.

He determined lives of all living things and guaranteed their sustenance, gave them bodies out of nothing.

Nobody understands my soul, no one can tell me anything about my soul, it is the order of my God, brings my body alive.

Let me explain my remaining senses: The reality is to do good for people by opening your inner eyes and looking to them, listening to them and hearing with your inner ears, looking to them and attaining their secrets.

My knowledge is not of today; if you know, it is a very old divine order, a verse.

Wisdoms of questions and answers were told until now, there is no end to what is after this.

Your share with Yunus is thus far. The heart is the stop of the true friend, and my mouth tells of him and witnesses.

BECOME ONE

Abandon duality and become one, come to this door dead, give up your life so that you would find the eternal life.

If you are worried about losing your life, if you think that you have life and obey your life, you would be left alone with your ego.

What countless wishes there are in this world! One day, a journey takes place, and nobody stays here. This is the ordain of the fate, you would die at the end of this path.

If you do not die of your longing for him, you cannot reach the cure. If you sacrifice your life for him, spend and consume this life for him, you will get a thousand lives. If you wear this skin dress out for him and take it off, you will get a thousand bodies to wear.

Do not fall for temporary desires, do not look to worldly jewels wishfully, you would find hidden treasures in hundred thousand worlds. Search for the Truth and see the Truth in every creature you find beautiful, so that you would reach to the reality of the shadow.

Those who do not look with love look to the image, cannot go beyond the image; they cannot reach to the meaning, they think appearances as real beauties. If you have a taste of love with your inner lips, you will go beyond outer looks and reach to the meaning; then you would be freed from the fire of apartness.

O, Yunus! Where is your mind, look, your mouth speaks without knowing, unintentionally, there is no end to this path, where are you strolling?

GOD GAVE ME SUCH A HEART

The Truth gave me such a heart, it admires him without even saying his name; sometimes it cheers up, sometimes, it cries.

Sometimes you think it is winter, like it is February; sometimes it rises from humanity with spring, becomes a garden.

Sometimes it does not say anything, cannot explain a word; sometimes it speaks out pearly words, becomes remedy for distressed.

Sometimes it goes up over the highest skies, sometimes it goes down under the lowest grounds; sometimes you think it is a drop, sometimes it overflows, becomes a sea.

Sometimes it is left in ignorance, becomes unable to recognize any object; sometimes it dives into seas, becomes Galen and Luqman; finds remedy for every suffering.

Sometimes it becomes a giant or a fairy; sometimes it flies with the Queen of Sheba, becomes the ruler of men and jinn.

Sometimes it makes the dead alive like Jesus; sometimes it goes into an arrogant state, becomes a vizier with Pharaoh.

Sometimes it turns to Gabriel, spreads mercy in every state; sometimes it loses its way, poor Yunus becomes an admirer.

PROPER WORDS

All the meanings I find about you in my heart, my mouth will tell these, it will speak of these ever. Wherever I go, my purpose is always to reach you. My path shall not draw away from you.

It is correct if I call those who do not love you deads; those who are alive with a living heart need a beloved like you.

You said you are behind a veil and cannot be seen to everybody; if you walk without a curtain for a moment in two worlds those who see you would perish.

People, angels, and all living creatures love you; they admire your beauty, houris and angels petrify before you.

It tastes like honey to me even if I drink poison from your hands, I don't know what meaning that drink has? But they enliven me, suffering and ordeal coming from you. They do not hurt me because they come from you; I would be happy even if I do not know where they come from, my soul needs those.

If I eat honey and sugar without you, without remembering you, they become poison for my soul. You are the enjoyment of my soul, everything I eat, and drink becomes tasty and give enjoyment to my soul by remembering you. Is it possible to call something that only gives taste to the tongue a dessert?

If I be subject to torture and suffering a hundred thousand times; I would never stop being consent with you, loving you is far worth all my miseries.

Yet, the existence of Yunus is just a particle within love. Safety of the lands and the skies, rotation of the universe, circulation of the destiny are all for the sake of love.

I SPENT THIS LIFE FOR NOTHING

I had spent this life of mine for nothing without thinking what I was living for, without knowing the true purpose of living; therefore, I had deserved to be thrown into the fire and burn.

I had done such an evil that no one would do to anyone to myself without even knowing what it is.

I collected the things I did and took them with me, I saw that I did not do anything useful; I had worked at a loss all my life.

I had carelessly committed sins to get a broken vase in the world and to achieve my wishes.

All I did in my life was vanity, how strange it is, I had forgotten righteousness and sincerity.

No one knows if they will make it to the night, I had forgotten death and fell into desires and wishes.

I followed my ego and spent my life for its desires and wishes, my loss is evident of that, what have I done.

Desperate Yunus has a lot of sins; there is only one to lead me to my salvation and I had rubbed my face onto the threshold of his lodge.

I FOUND THE ONE WITHIN ME

I found the one within me, let this life of mine be looted. I gave up profit, loss, and all kinds of benefits, let my shop be looted.

I gave up my ego, opened the veil on my eyes, reached my true friend, let my doubts be looted.

My desire to exist was gone, the true friend covered all my possessions; I became free from space, let my space be looted.

I broke with everything, flew towards that true friend, fell into the assembly of love, let my assembly be looted.

I am tired of duality, satisfied with the feast of unity, burning with the desire to rejoin, reached the pleasure of love's misery by enduring its troubles, let my cure be looted.

To be reflected in the world of existence, the true friend came to us from him, my ruined heart was filled with divine light, let my existence be looted.

I said stop to my desires and wishes, gave up all of them. I got tired from the enjoyment of summer and the hardship of winter. I found the garden of roseries, my secret garden, let my gardens be looted.

Yunus, how nice you have told, like tasting honey and sugar. I found the honey of honeys let my hive be looted.

DESTINATION OF THIS PATH IS FAR

The destination of this path is far, whoever sets off on this path; there are many challenges down the path, whoever wants to accomplish this.

Those need to do many preparations before setting off on this path, complete all their shortcomings, be brave, whoever sets off on this path.

It is narrow like the bridge between heaven and hell, they need to pass through this path; righteousness and honesty are the only solutions for those who are heading to the true friend.

Whoever has righteousness and honesty, the Truth loves those; it will be valid in both worlds, the capital of those brave people.

The stone of repentance and praying for forgiveness was thrown with the catapult of righteousness, the ego fortress was demolished.

Know that those who misguide people are abundant on this path, disgrace of those who go with their egos does not go away.

There are hundreds of thousands hypocrisy soldiers on this path, brave people who killed their egos are needed to decimate those soldiers.

Yunus now they knell, let us give up our lives and head to absence; if your eyes are worthy, see the beauty of the true friend.

THE DRINK FROM THE TRUTH

We drank the drink coming from the Truth, thank God we dived and passed through the meanings of this sea of might, thanks to God.

We healthily and happily overcame those mountains, forests, gardens, and all the challenges we faced by working hard, thanks to God.

We had water when we were dry, our heart revived when we were dead, we found life, got wings, and became birds; we enthused and got freed from the captivity of the body, coupled up with each other and flew, thanks to God.

We spread the meaning of Baba Tapduk as life to the hearts in the cities we visited, thanks to God.

Come near let us make peace, get to know each other. Our horse is saddled, our preparations are complete, our ego is disciplined, we set off and ran, thanks to God.

We went down to the land of Rum, we spent the winter, we served and did many good deeds. There came the spring and we migrated back, thanks to God.

Our hearts woke up and we revived, we spoke out of our hearts and became spring, we rejoined with those with knowledge and wisdom like a great sea and became a stream, we poured into that sea of might and got filled, thanks to God.

We stood before Tapduk and became a servant at his door; poor Yunus was raw, not yet ripened, we matured, thanks to God.

BE A SERVANT TO A SULTAN

Be servant to such a sultan of hearts that has never been dethroned or discharged. Set your heart on such a threshold that no one can take away from you.

You should fly like a bird and overcome many obstacles. You should retreat and drink a juice of love; those who drank should never got sober, should stay drunk.

Like an agile duck, you should dive into a sea; extract an ore that not every goldsmith can recognize.

You should enter a garden, walk inside, and get refreshed. You should smell a fresh rose that was reddened with the fire of love will never fade.

You also should fall in love, get to know your beloved. To never burn in any fire again, you should burn with the fire of love.

You also should get to know the Truth, hear from the Truth. You should die here before death so that you will never die again.

Yunus! Sit calmly, now, turn your face towards the Creator. Give rise to a brave man like your essence who was never born.

STATE OF THIS WORLD

State of this world is like a big city; our life is like a small marketplace.

Everybody come to this city, stay for a while; their return is like a one-way journey.

The life in this city is sweeter than sugar-syrup at first; when the youth pass by it becomes like a snake poison with its pains and aches.

In the beginning it indulges with its beauties, in the end as you get older it turns away and becomes like a trickster old woman.

Boundless dreams a plenty in this city; those who fall for these dreams and get deceived become like witches.

This city has a sultan who gives donations to everybody; those who get to know this sultan become like they exist while they really do not.

Those who know their places, know their own states; Friends of God never get old with love, they are like the approaching spring.

See desperate Yunus, he became an admirer of the true friend through his grieves; every breath of him is like sugar-syrup.

IF YOU ASK ABOUT THE TRUE FRIEND

If you ask about the true friend, then know that his words are not baseless and has deep meanings; his deeds are noteworthy. Be aware that anyone devoid of the true friend in this world is nothing.

Whoever sees the face of the true friend in this world consumes his life thinking about the true friend. And if he dies while still thinking about the true friend, then he unites with that true friend and forgets about any confusion and disorder except for the true friend.

Whoever finds a path towards the true friend invites everyone to him. I attained a state thanks to the true friend, so I no longer need worldly ranks or positions.

The true friend tests and surprises man many times. At the end, his vessels of power float on the sea of soul of those sincere and loyal. The dead ones with still hearts may only see in their dreams; come and interpret these dreams.

The universe is filled with the love of the true friend; hearts came alive with him; he was remembered through him; flowers bloomed without love faded and died. The true friend may only be consented with love and affection.

How may I tell about him; no one can understand this; where can I find a value to describe him? There is no touchstone to indicate his value like the one measuring the value of gold.

A lover who loves love and who will live love for the sake of love; admit living love as his sole purpose and have no other purpose is required. What could be higher than love! Love is the pillar of the universe, the earth, and the sky; everything else is a vain promise.

Yunus! Now that you are me; the lovers do not need you and me. There is only the true friend for them; those who love the true friend are in nothingness, and they do not have a different sight.

I USED TO TRAVEL ON THE EARTH

I used to travel on the Earth; I saw many people in the cities lying; some were nobles, and some were brave men.

Some were young, some were old; some were viziers, and some were teachers; their daylights turned into nights; there are many of them lying in the dark pits.

They used to have straight paths; they were literates; they spoke like nightingales; the wise and brave men lie.

The strong brave men tumbled down, the noble ones cried; they lie with their broken bows and arrows erected by their heads.

The glorious men who used to walk with fanfare and fame, who used to rise clouds of dust, and who used to have authority over the states lie.

The youngsters who used to sing like nightingales during the day and night closed their eyes to this world; and those whose mothers are crying by their graves lie.

Beautiful, graceful, and tall women who had hennas on their hands and who had pretty maids lie.

All have their hands tied and are hopeful of God. Some of those lying are young maids or little children.

Yunus does not know about his state, God makes him speak; some of those who lie are recently wed brides or those with white and clean faces.

THE STATION OF LOVE IS SUPREME

The station of love is supreme; love is eternal. The words spoken by the lovers are the words of the Truth. It is only the tongue of might that talks about love.

It is him to speak, to hear, to see, and to show. That appearance speaking every word is where all living beings want to reach.

The shape or the mouth has no words to speak unless the meaning arrives. What is spoken is the Truth himself and his meaning. The meaning of the Truth is spoken; tongue is the path of wisdom.

This is our job; this is our pleasure; the syrup that we drink and enjoy comes from the lake of love; it is the discourse of the true friend that we listen to and enjoy.

If you wish to remember that beloved, it is again him to tell it; the words belong to him. He is ours and we are his; this is the language of glorification.

The one who honestly believes in God has never found a lie in the works of Yunus. Those who are not enlightened with these words, those who spend their lives in darkness are deprived of this consciousness and talent.

GOD! GIVE ME LOVE

God! Give me such a love that I forget about myself; such a love that I lose myself, such that I do not find myself even if I want to.

Dazzle me so that I lose track of time; may You be the only one that I ask for such that I am not mistaken by other images.

Take me and remove this ego from me and fill me in with you. Allow me to die before that so that I won't die again.

Let my heart speak with your love. I don't care if anyone curses me or laughs at me. Let me burn down with my grief and never tell anyone about my state.

I am walking in fire with my heart torn out. Enough! What this love has done to this soul! How may I not cry?

My soul smelled that divine scent of you. It could not stand longing for you anymore and abandoned every worldly thing. However, your location is unknown, where should I ask for you?

May I become a nightingale and sing; may I land on the garden of the true friend. May I become a rose and never fade away.

Let them put me on the gallows like Mansoor; just then, remove the veils and show yourself. Let me sacrifice this soul rather than being a denier or hypocrite.

The remedy of my suffering is love; I am ready to sacrifice myself for the sake of love; Yunus Emre speaks these words as long as I am not left without love again.

I SPENT MY DAYS IN VAIN

I have spent my days in vain without worshipping, following the orders of the creator or doing charities. O, my life! What shall I do with it?

I failed to realize that it passed by. I didn't have the chance to cry and worry about my state. I never wanted to abandon you. O, my life! What shall I do with it?

The good and evil I do are recorded on my book by the scripting angles. My life is consumed day by day; my appearance and my body decay. O, my life! What shall I do with it?

When you are consumed, you do not come back. You may not find me again, because you are the capital of this ego. O, my life! What shall I do with it?

I considered and trusted you to be endless; I tried hard to rejoice and live a good life. All my earnings and savings are left behind. O my life! What shall I do with it?

Poor Yunus! You are on this long journey; you stay away from the world with longing. O my life! What shall I do with it?

IF YOU NEED A LESSON

If you want to draw a lesson in the world, go and visit those graves in the cemeteries. Even a rock would melt down upon seeing them.

They were wealthy when they were alive, but they were gone by leaving all behind. Look, what they became now! Eventually, they wore a collarless white shirt which neither had sleeves.

Where are the ones claiming to have wealth and those turning their noses up at the mansions and palaces? They are now lying the graves made of soil and covered with stones.

They used to have fun they and night; they never came home or performed their worships. They may no longer find that splendor again. Those days are all gone.

Where are those who speak nice words? Where are the beautiful ones with faces bright like the sun? They all decayed and lost in the soil, and no sign of their beauties left.

Those in the graves were once governors, they used hire servants but now, look what they have turned into! You may not distinguish governors from the servants.

There is neither door to enter in, no food to eat not a light to see in the graves. Their daylights turned into nights.

Yunus you will also leave all your belongings behind one day! You will be just like the others.

O FRIEND! THE FIRE OF YOUR LOVE

O, the true friend! The fire of you love tears my heart out; I burn with your love, and this burning pleases me.

As I am burning with the love of fire, my laughter has turned into crying. O, the true friend! My yearning and burning for you is repellent for the deniers.

If I explain why I am burning with this love, it would be misunderstood and lead to a fight. But, if I do not tell, then I may not feel comfortable and that would tear my heart out. The world is full of traitors; they first listen and share, then when it does not suit their books, each one says a word and I take a hit on my head.

Look, what they tell me and how they stone me! I endure all for the sake of the true friend! Those words hit the heart like an arrow; yet some others who understand us come and share the same state with us.

O, the one who knows about us! We are not the deniers of love; who we love through the images is the Truth, but they appear like faces to people.

Many sultans lost themselves in love and become helpless and weak. Whoever sets off on this journey, joins this journey calmly and slowly.

The saints passed by this world without staying. Everybody is brothers and sisters to those who honestly love the Truth.

Poor Yunus, be aware of your words and open your eyes to the true friend. Just like the Sun becoming obvious in every creature with its colors, that beloved would also be seen through his attributes, behaviors, and states wherever you look at.

THE GRAVEYARD IN THE MORNING

I went to the graveyard in the morning and I saw everyone lying death, all were helpless, and all consumed their lives.

I got closer to them, and I took a look at the grandeur of death. Many young men were lying death before even attaining their desires.

The insects and worms had eaten their flesh, and there were holes on the chests of some. There were little children and pale youngsters lying death.

Their bodies fell prey to death, and their souls reached to God. Don't you see what is this about? They are lying death to indicate that the time of death will come for us too.

They lost their pearl-like teeth and their blond hair. Their worldly concerns are over. They are lying upon the order of God.

The light of their eyes dimmed; they do not have the effort to do anything. They spent the money they saved for the burial cloth, and now, they lie wrapped with that cloth.

Yunus, if you are a true lover, do not consume your life for wealth. Those who spent their lives for wealth are now lying in the arms of mother earth.

IF I TELL YOU MY SECRET

If I tell you my secret, nobody will understand my words. If I am patient and don't tell, then my heart will not consent me keeping silent.

O, the smart! O, the nobles! You tell me, what shall I do? Ever since I have seen the face of the true friend, I may not come to my senses.

I may not finish my work in this order; the affairs of the world never end. If my life ends and my works are half finished, then my soul completes its duty and my soul never leaves anything incomplete.

I am neither insane nor fully san. What does my state correspond with? I have dived into the sea of love; my heart and my soul never get enough.

This fire of affection burns within my heart as I remember my beloved. If I dive into the sea of love, only then that fire may die out; I don't make a mistake.

This rose of love blossoms within the fire twelve months a year. The more I burn inside, the more my fears grow. I hope my time does not pass by and my rose withers away.

All lovers turned towards the Truth and attained the Truth with patience. The essence of love is fire and I do not have patience for it.

Many times, I told to my heart to be patient and to keep quiet. It does not listen to my advice and gets even worse.

If this body of Yunus dies and becomes soil, the love within me never fades away.

EVERYBODY TALKS ABOUT MY LOVE TO YOU

Everybody talks about my love to You; let them talk whatever they want. I may not live without you. Even my life has no benefit to me without You.

Whoever fails to get Your taste walks like a dead body without receiving any news from or worries about this meaning.

I have just seen You. How may I be patient? Everybody would die to see You even for once.

The one who sees You does not need the beautiful servants or mansions in the heaven. Any place would be hell to a soul that does not love You.

Even if they give me the wealth of both worlds, what shall I do with them without You? My every deed becomes complete only with You.

Even if I had thousand lives, I would consume all for Your sake. If I am a true lover, let me die for you sake.

When all I need is You, what shall I do with my own self? If I willingly become You, then let me destroy myself.

The worlds desire You by burning and groaning because they want to find you. Since I have found You, how may I be without You?

Many people ask Yunus what kind of intoxication of love is this? What else he can do; this is how the pen wrote his destiny when the souls were created.

I PUT MY FACE ON THE GROUND

If now I put my face on the ground before you, a new moon will rise on the skies of my heart at any moment; every moment feels like a festival to me. My summer and my winter will turn into the spring.

The clouds may not leave the light of my moon in shadow; it never loses its integrity, and it shines brightly. My moon is on the ground and its divine light rises from the ground to the skies and rains down on heaven.

His divine light enlightens and removes the darkness in the hearts of those who are looking at him. How may darkness and the divine light be in the same place at the same time!

I saw my moon, my glamorous beloved on the ground. What would I ask from the sky? The mercy pours on my face from the ground.

This word of mine is not for the moon or the day; I am using this metaphor to describe my beloved to the lovers. If I fail to describe, the suffering of love suffocates me.

What if Yunus loved! The Truth has many lovers, and His lovers burn inside. He answers to their love and accepts them.

ABSENCE AND POVERTY

Those who became a friend of God found it in absence and poverty by abandoning all their wealth without relying on their properties. Those who act in a conceited manner tumbled down the stairs if they looked down on others with arrogance.

The heart inclines upwards, therefore, it strays away with every moment; whatever a man has inside acts out.

An old teacher with white beard, yet with an unknown state, should not make effort to go to pilgrimage if he has broken a heart. The heart is the house of God; because, God said, "I may not fit into nowhere but into the heart of my beloved servant." Anyone stoning that house may never be improved.

The one whose inner ears are deaf may not hear these words. The bling one mistakes day for night. The eyes of a denier may not see even if the world is bright.

The heart is the house of the Truth; the Truth looked into the heart. Anyone who breaks such a heart would be unhappy in both worlds.

Consider the others the way you think about yourself. This is the meaning of four scriptures if they are understood.

The people we knew have passed by and those who settled into this world returned to their homelands. Whoever heard the meaning with the inner ears, whoever watched the beauty with the inner eyes, and whoever tastes with the inner lips drank from the wine of love.

O, Yunus! Those who stray away may not reach higher levels or attain nice stations. May those who love the Truth be saved from the torture in the grave.

HEAR ME, MY FRIENDS!

Hear me, my friends! Love is like a sun. It enlightens everything and everywhere without discriminating or distinguishing the beautiful from the ugly. A heart that does not burn with the fire of love is like a solid rock.

No plants grow on rocks. The same applies to the heart. It may not produce any good feelings. The tongues of the stonyhearted people are poisonous. Whatever they tell disturb people and lead to a discussion or fight even if they make effort to say it softly and calmly. Their words are like wars.

Those who have love burn and yearn for the beloved. Their hearts are soft and melt like a burning candle. The stonyhearted people who have not get their shares from love yet have dark faces and their hearts are like harsh winter.

He stands by the door of that sultan before the Truth; he is the leading star of the lovers, and he is like a sergeant training the lovers.

Abandon your worries, Yunus! Do not think and be concerned about those who will cross your path! You first need love in this journey to reach your goal; the one with love is like a humble dervish.

DON'T YOU REMEMBER THAT DAY

Don't you remember that day? When the day comes, the soul flies away from the body, your eyes see nothing, and your tongue speaks nothing.

Azrael arrives and pulls the soul away; no one may endure his imposing appearance. The flutters of your parents won't help, or the people won't come to rescue.

The officer is notified, and he announces your death to your friends and enemies. Now, pull yourself together, abandon your mistakes; otherwise, there is no point crying over spilt milk.

First, the person to wash your body and his assistants come. Then, the person to put your burial cloth on arrives. None of them knows about your state.

They put you in the coffin, take you to the grave and descend you under the ground. They cover you and leave you alone. No one sees you again.

They talk about you a couple of days, then they share and distribute all your belongings. Then, no one remembers you.

Poor Yunus, you'd better give this advice to yourself first! People these days do not benefit from this advice.

WHEREVER I TURN TO

Wherever I turn to and wherever I look at, I occupy myself with love; my job is love. Love is what boils within my heart, and love is my companion.

I feel pity for those without love. I reveal my secrets to convince and give them love. I do not refrain from being misunderstood, and I share my experiences. When I see the lovers, I overflow with enthusiasm.

This love is a grace to us, and it is the dearest to us. Whatever we live for, we do it for the sake of love and we defend love. That's why I am in a war with the satan.

I came, saw, and watched the world. I told to myself that I would leave any day now. I don't want to spend too much time here; I may not be together with the one I desire in this world; I may not finish my work in this world.

Yunus says, "I am both in love and loyal to my love and beloved. I have found what I was looking for; I do not have anything to search for with pleasure and joy like other lovers."

HOW MAY I HIDE THAT I LOVE

How may I hide that I love the beloved. His love does not fit into my heart, what shall I do? At least, let me tell his name encoded.

Walking around holding my tongue without mentioning about you estranges me from my beloved. Let me burn down that veil of estrangement, declare my love and be saved from being ashamed.

Let me announce my state with him to the worlds. Let me invite and herald everyone to be with me.

The eyes and hearts of the lovers are turned towards the beloved; may I make my heart his servant and reach the beloved.

Let me sacrifice myself to him if he accepts my life; I will die anyway, then why should I be still alive!

It would be a great pleasure if I die for the sake of the true friend; we will eventually die; I will at least die for the sake of the true friend and reach the true friend.

Actually, the interrogation angels are the very own deeds of the people. My only occupation was the true friend, I was only busy with remember him. So, let me take my deeds with me.

What Yunus tells about is not the affection for knowledge and worship. The tongue would not know about the true friend; these words come from my unity with the true friend. I tell news about the true friend.

LET'S ASK THE SOULS

Let's ask the souls what happened to their bodies, how did the body decay? It was claiming to be all yours, but what caused the body to get out your hands?

Look, the body is leaving. This is not a lie/mistake; this is the truth itself. The soul heard from the true friend asking it to come to him. It is going by abandoning the body.

What about his properties and wealth? He abandoned all of it! He appears before the sultan of the worlds by taking the records on his book of deeds.

If the soul found the true friend, then it means everything is right. When such a soul is abandoning the body, it smiles at his corpse lying on the ground and says farewell.

It used to walk around the shops and did anything for a small amount of money! It has had fill of this world and leaves by putting on the shroud which is a collarless shirt.

Thousands of people are born and thousands of them leave; it seems that this is how it is commanded. Those who do not feel affection to this world leaves by filling their cups with love.

They discourse day and night by wishing to find the Truth. Yunus says, the poor one has found the Truth here.

THE ARROW OF LOVE

O, the true friend! Your sharp eyes are the arrows of love and it influences even the coldest hearts. Those who are caught by your love leaves their lives behind.

Those who worry about you cry day and night and become the lovers of your love. They do not worry about anything else and leave all the hesitations and turmoil behind.

The hearts of those who fall into your love burn. Those who give themselves to you leave all their occupation behind.

The love for this world is like a poisonous food. Those thinking of the other world give up eating that poisonous food.

The smart ones do not worship for heaven or at a charge. They do not fall for beautiful maids and renounce their beauties.

The true lovers hurry to die and reach the beloved; if they had a thousand head, they would give up each one to reach the true friend.

This world is like an illusion or a dream to the wise men. Those who dedicate themselves to you, abandon this illusion and dream.

Yunus is full of love for the Truth; he moves away from all his friends and relatives to be alone with the Truth.

THE ONE ASKING FOR THE TRUTH

O, the one asking for the Truth day and night! Don't you know where the Truth is? He is present wherever you are. He is there wherever you look at.

Don't wish the Truth to be away from you. The station of the Truth is in the heart. Abandon and leave your ego behind. He is inside your body, in your soul.

Enter in and look into your heart, he is there. Abandon your ego, find that pure ore. Do not suppose that it is in the seas far away.

Thousands of ore became worthless than a particle in that sea. It is not possible to tell that soul has disappeared. The soul to disappear is in the animal.

He knows about your image. The secret of soul reaches him. The inner eyes see the truth of the true friend, the bodily eyes are far away.

Yunus Emre! Open your eyes and take a look. Both worlds are filled with the Truth. Everywhere is covered with his attributes. Burn your suspicions with faith. He is not hidden, but evident.

FOR THE SAKE OF THE TRUTH

My soul suffers for the Truth. Are there any sufferings other than or worse than longing for you?

Everybody witnessed that the fire of your love burns in my heart. Wherever someone burns, it is seen because of the smoke.

Your love sent soldiers to occupy the house of my heart. It took my soul captive. No enemy can do anything to me.

Let me send news to all countries and let me speak my last words to all lovers; may they beware the beloved because he plays with the heart of the lover.

I wonder why there is no remedy found to my suffering. Who keeps the one to heal my suffering away from me?

The sultans of love have rules; when their slaves commit a sin, they discipline them or sell the slave in the market.

Yunus, do not complain about enduring the sufferings from the beloved. The desire of all lovers ends up before that beloved.

O, BEAUTY! BE GENEROUS

O, beauty! Be generous and look towards this way. Remove the veil from your face. Your face shines bright like the moon with your ruddy cheeks.

May you be allowed to tell us the truth from that beautiful mouth with hundred thousand praises.

The pureness of your face is so attractive, your brows are like the crescent, your forehead is brighter than the moon.

How may those who see the light on your face keep away from falling into the fire like a dragonfly? The look in your eyes claims lives; it is brighter than fire.

The lovers tied from their necks with the melody of your love never want to be relieved. They willingly remained captive.

Which of your beauties may the tongue speak of? You'd better stay away from all the eyes.

Your neck may not be distinguished from the neck of a gazella, your eyes are like a gazella's eyes; you are so beautiful like nothing on earth. I recognized you just I was about to ask whether it was you; those ears with earrings brought me into doubt.

This lover, Yunus, saw the manifestation of the Truth on your face. No way; I may not break up with you anymore; I may not leave you; because the Truth appeared to me from you.

I AM IN A WONDROUS STATE

I fell into a wondrous state because of this love; I may not see ahead of me, I may not walk on the street because of this love.

While everyone in the world praised me and treated me with great respect, I became miserable and fell on the ground; now, everybody vilifies me because of this love.

Like a lonely nightingale, I travel and cry by remembering my beloved. I shed flood of tears because of this love.

My face turned pale like dry leaves; may I grow pale and die because of this love.

May I tear my collar on the Judgment Day and shout out because of this love.

What if I reach my beloved from now on! I got old, I buckled up, and I lost my youth because of your love.

Yunus! Pray for your Tapduk. Never say what shall I do because of this love.

COME ON, MY HEART!

Come on, my heart! Walk comfortably and in peace for some time; do not be afraid of or refrain from anyone. Trust in the Truth and walk free from sorrow and worry.

If you want to see the reality, your ego is enough for you as an enemy; now, go and fight, battle, struggle with your ego.

It is the ego that lets a man down; the one who follows the ego is stranded. Do not occupy yourself with others. You should not get angry with other, but yourself.

If you want to be safe from the evil of this world, abandon this grudge and arrogance. Content yourself with what is enough to keep your body and soul together like a dervish. Work hard and earn; but be humble and contented.

If you want to be drunk in this world and be happy forever, fill in your cup of love and be drunk by drinking twelve months of the year.

Do not enter the yard or field of affection of anyone! Do not speak about anyone's heart or beloved! Go and be happy with your beloved in your own garden of love.

Do not darken the hearts or do not lead to unrest in the discourses through immature behaviors. Immature things are tasteless; come and mature on the fire of love.

Yunus, now you say nice things and tell the secrets of love to your listeners. Give advice to people. Walk on the path of the Truth and reach Him.

MY LOVE FOR THE CREATOR

The love for my Creator fell into my heart and made a wound in my heart. It took my heart and disclosed my secret.

He never leaves my heart and I keep on talking about Him. I speak about him and mention him all the time. My Creator showed his divine light to me and pleased me.

My inner eyes saw him, and my tongue spoke about him to me unwittingly. He came and settled into my heart. He made my heart his throne.

He offered a cup to my soul and my soul drank from it thirstily. The cups filled in and made my soul drunk.

Our soul became drunk with his wine of love. Our tongue speaks beautiful words like pearls. The love of my Creator intoxicated me.

When shall I be a candidate to reach him? He made hundred thousand of people like me candidates to him by allowing them to wear the coat of love.

Yunus rejoices and consoles thinking that he has seen the true friend. He overflew in the assembly of Sufi saints and reveled.

MAN OF MEANING ON THIS PATH

The man of meaning will not be sad on this path, those hearts that have heard the meaning will never die.

The body is temporary, the soul is immortal, those who went away from this world will not return; it is the body that dies, souls will not die.

Even the hearts that love jewels go to a place hundred thousand miles away if the Truth doesn't predestine it they will not attain it.

The heart of the beloved is a silver coated glass you should never break it! If the silver coated glass is broken it will not become a whole again.

If you leave your glass under a fountain without filling it; it will not fill itself even if it stays there for a thousand years.

This Khizr, this Elijah, they drank the water of immortality; they will not die even if years pass by.

The Truth created the world for the sake of Mohammad's friendship; those who come to the world pass away, they will not stay forever.

Yunus while your eyes are still seeing, make your preparations today; those who went there did not come back, they never will.

IF YOU LOVE THE LOVE

If you love and want love, you should be breath to the souls. You should find a remedy to and be cure for everyone's sufferings.

If you love the world, then you will be addicted to it; if you get lost in pleasure and delight, how may you attain the secret of the meaning?

The world is an old, ruined palace and you are the master of it. How may you fancy such a life and poison your future? You have forgotten your purpose of creation and enjoying yourself in palaces; you are risking your endless life in the future by consuming your life with temporary beauties of the world.

You are left like a bird without wings in the foreign lands of this world. How may you reach the Sufi saints who spread their wings and fly towards the meaning?

A friend of God should give you a cane so that you find your way with that cane just like the blind person trailing with a cane.

This word of Yunus is for those with nice hearts. If you attain the meaning of these words and become a lover, then you will wake up.

IF YOU'VE MET A MIGHTY PERSON

If you have met a mighty person, why are you still concerned about the beauty of the face? Look at his breathtaking beauty sincerely with your inner eyes; what will you do with the beauty of the face? If you have found the way to dive into the meaning, then what would you do with the worldly affairs?

Abandon being excessively keen on the worldly blessings; you may not attain the meaning because of them. Come and enter the fire of love, reach farther. Do not fall behind.

The primary materials of this body are fire, water, earth, and air. Eventually, each one of them returns to their origin. Earth returns to earth; water to water; fire to fire; and air to air. Wake up and see the reality! Do not be heedless.

The houses of idols and wineries turned into prayer rooms for the true soul. The place does not matter to worship God as long as you are honest and refrain from hypocrisy! Do not be a liar.

As you are a traveler on the path to the afterlife, abandon the love for this transitory life. If you are in love, then what is your love for wealth?

You are claiming to own many things. The Truth is the owner of all the properties, isn't he? Are you going into a partnership with him? The Sultan would forgive your guilt, but what about going astray?

You are concerned about being poor day and night. Your Lord is generous, He would give you your subsistence. Why are you concerned?

Eat and offer to the poor; if you consume all, the Creator will give you again. One day, your body goes into the earth. Then, what are those you left behind?

Yunus, you drank wine of love from that jar of love and became drunk! You attained the Truth when you were deprived of him. What is being sober to the Truth?

I CRY FOR THE TRUE FRIEND

If I miss and cry because of my longing to the true friend, who will console me and wipe away my tears? Because these tears keep on coming with such a mourning and groaning.

O, the lovers! O, brothers! Who shall I explain my state? Who shall I ask for a remedy for my suffering? Who shall I go? Who knows about it?

Even if the entire world is a remedy, it may not cure me without you. How can it cure me without you because my heart only loves the true friend.

If I die and go into the grave, do not let my flesh and body to decay. Do not allow me to be separated from my beloved because I am going to the beloved.

In the realm of spirits, I was him and he was me before even we were asked "Am I not your Lord?" How could this be forgotten? How could one stop hoping from him?

My friends and my brothers ask me why they haven't seen me recently. Because my body fell apart, I travel from one destination to another.

My relationship with that true friend will not end even if I die. How may it end! Because that true friend is loved by this heart.

Tomorrow, when the Judgment Day arrives, all the servants will be preoccupied with their own selves. But, I never think of Yunus, and speak of Tapduk all the time.

FARUK DİLAVER

A Sufi on the path of Yunus Emre

ABOUT THE AUTHOR

Faruk Dilaver was born in 1946 in Vezirköprü, a county of Samsun. He completed elementary school in Vezirköprü, secondary school in Tokat, high school in Ordu, and his higher education at Eskişehir Economics and Commercial Sciences Academy. He also received computer education in Germany and England.

He provided significant services for the introduction and establishment of computers in Turkey and trained many experts in this field. After serving in the Air Force for eleven years, he administered a foundation establishment subsidiary to Hacettepe University. Following that duty, he pioneered in the establishment and was the chairman of the board of four companies in the computer business.

After thirty years of business life, he devoted the rest of his life to research and spread Yunus Emre's thoughts and cultures by establishing Yunus Emre Culture and Social Aid Association. Parallel to his studies, he produced many works, and three of his works have been translated into English.

He is still giving speeches at seminars and conferences in Turkey and abroad in the direction of Yunus Emre's ideas of love, unity, and peace. Faruk Dilaver is married and a father of two children.

Printed in Great Britain
by Amazon